SEASONAL CYCLES

SEASONAL CYCLES

A STUDY OF SOCIAL CHANGE AND CONTINUITY IN A SRI LANKAN VILLAGE

VICTOR C. DE MUNCK
DEPARTMENT OF ANTHROPOLOGY
UNIVERSITY OF CALIFORNIA, RIVERSIDE

GYAN

Published by

Gyan Publishing House
5, Ansari Road
Daryaganj, New Delhi-110002
Phone: 011-47034999, 9811692060
E-mail: books@gyanbooks.com

Distribution Network
gyanbooks.com
India, USA, Canada, UK, Australia, France

ISBN : 978-81-212-3987-5 (PB)
First Published, New Delhi 1993

2nd Impression 2020

Printed at: Gyan Press, Delhi.

Seasonal Cycles
Author: Victor C. De Munck

ACKNOWLEDGEMENT

Bound between the covers of this monograph are the voices, support, guidance and affection of many people. First of all I dedicate this book to my mother and in the memory of my father whose love and help extended beyond any expression of thanks.

It was while sitting in on a lecture by Frederick G. Bailey at the University of California at San Diego that my interest in anthropology was first sparked. It was in Gananath Obeyesekere's classroom that I determined that Sri Lanka was to be the country where I wanted to do fieldwork. The intelligence, inquisitiveness and humanity of these two mentors have served as models by which to guide my own work.

Gananath provided invaluable assistance during my residence in Sri Lanka and serendipitously helped select Kotabowa as the location for my research. During my graduate years in anthropology at the University of California at Riverside, my academic training was guided by David Kronenfeld and Alan Beals. David gave sage counsel while Alan provided the theoretical tools which shape much of this text.

I owe a further debt to my wife, Trini Garro, who helped edit, draw the kinship diagrams, and supported and encouraged me every step of the way.

In Sri Lanka there are numerous people who need to be acknowledged. Lal Weerakkody and his family took me into their home on my arrival in Sri Lanka. I quickly became a part of the family and Lal and I remain "ambe yaluwo" (or best "friends").

To the villagers of Kotabowa (a pseudonym) I extent my deepest thanks. The villagers were always hospitable to me and sympathetic towards my research. I hope that my affection for the villagers is reflected in these pages. The *Grama Sevaka* (village headman), Mr. Suraweera, volunteered his time and knowledge to me throughout my stay. My field assistant, Mr. "Singer" Muthulingam was also a fortunate "find." His easy camaraderie, understanding of my objectives and ability to phrase questions and elicit "intimate" details enriched both my research and residence in Kotabowa. To Salaam (the school-master), Farook, Siddik, Hamsa, Latif, Hadji, Ishmael, the *Marikar*, Waeda Mahatteya, the *Lebbe*, the Trustee, Nauman and Ibrahim Maulevi and others, I extend my heartfelt thanks and friendship.

TABLE OF CONTENTS

LIST OF TABLES

LIST OF FIGURES

INTRODUCTION

Theory and Method

I view culture as comprised of purposive activities. The objective of an ethnographer is to describe and analyze these activities by asking two fundamental questions—what do people do and why do they do it? Culture is neither bounded nor static, but always in flux, in the process of change. These are not new observations, but they provide the crucible in which new theories and methods are developed, modified, or rejected.

Traditional ethnographers described and analyzed culture as localized and segmented into interdependent systems. Leach (1961), Obeyesekere (1967), Bailey (1960, 1967), Beals (1970), Brow (1978), and others have pointed out that anthropologists typically concerned themselves with developing ideational rather than behavioral models of culture. In such ethnographies, village organization is described in terms of ideal types. The behavioral regularities are pronounced as "social facts" with their own behavioral valence.

The contemporary interest in the pragmatics rather than the norms of behavior brought individuals rather than institutions into the limelight of study. Leach (1961) puts this approach into context by asking the rhetorical question, "Why should I be looking for some social entity other than the individuals of the community itself?"

Without showing how and under what conditions actual behavior either approximates or varies from the ideal, an ethnography presents people as "automata," their actions controlled by an abstract deity called culture or social structure. The traditional ethnographic model of describing cultures in terms of their component systems—i.e., religious, political, social, economic—has fallen into disrepute. Yet, for all the current concern with depicting the ethnographic context accurately, including on occasions the contextual effect of the ethnographer's presence (Srinivas 1976; Obeyesekere 1984; Shore 1984; Romanucci-Ross 1986), no alternative public model has been nominated for general ethnographic purposes. While in earlier ethnographies the people themselves are often absent having been sacrificed for holistic normative depictions of a community, contemporary ethnographies often sacrifice the whole for the part, focusing on one particular set of behaviors. As Tax expressed it, "...the problem oriented monograph, which has become fashionable, has virtually destroyed what was once the glory and value of the holistic monograph...(1976:vii)."

It is within this contrast set—the whole or the part, individual variability or behavioral regularities—that I have had to make my decisions. I have opted to compare behavioral regularities, presented as normative or ideational models, with individual variations in behaviors from these norms. The behavior of villagers is viewed as based on a calculus of accommodation between social norms and personal resources, strategies and psychological proclivities. These social norms can be translated into "should" statements. They do not compel or prescribe behavior but provide a recipe for behavior that has, more or less, worked in the past. They do, however, delineate the probable social consequences of actions as generalized to the population in question. The ethnographic task is to first define the cultural contexts and then to evaluate the behavioral responses of individuals acting within these contexts.

In the following section of this introduction I will show how I have incorporated this theoretical and methodological model into the organization of this ethnography.

Organization

Fieldwork was carried on in the Sri Lankan village of Kotabowa. Farmer (1957; 1977); Leach (1961), Obeyesekere (1967), Brow (1978) and Morrison, Moore and Lebbe (1979) noted that the traditional Sri Lankan village was integrated around rice cultivation with its associated cultural values of sharing and reciprocating alliances. The "disintegration" of the economic centrality of rice in favor of new capitalistic economic avenues discussed by Morrison, Moore and Lebbe, while apparent in Kotabowa, had not yet led to the replacement of the dominant economic status of paddy cultivation. As such, the pattern of village activities remained coordinated with the annual cycle of the weather. During the rainy season (*Maha*) villagers farmed, during the dry season villagers turned to other activities.

All able-bodied villagers participated, more or less, in seasonally associated activities. I identified three recognizable seasons: the *chena* (or swidden), paddy and festival season. There was overlap, but each season consisted of a series of distinct, integrated, sequential activities known to all villagers.

The *chena* season began in August–September, a month or so prior to the first rains; the paddy season commenced with the first rains in November or December; and the festival season began after the rice was harvested and winnowed, in April or May. The villagers' concerns, interests, energies and consequent activities were mobilized by these seasonal cycles. These divisions were never mutually exclusive, festivals occurred during both the *chena* and paddy seasons. But seasonal cycles, by and large, determined the pattern of activities villagers engaged in at a given time. Seasonal activity cycles are contingent on environmental conditions and given the absence of year around irrigation facilities all villagers organized their lives within these ecological parameters.

Each season consists of its own set of tasks, organizational principles, constraints, equipment, resources, sources of conflict, and goals. In a sense, the community itself can best be defined as those members who participate and share the same annual calendar of work. It is, ultimately, these shared sets of activities that identify the villagers of Kotabowa as members of a culture. When Morrison, Moore and Lebbe wrote of the "disintegrating" Sri Lankan villages, they indirectly referred to the disintegration of a village-shared seasonal cycle of activities. Figuratively, the end of a seasonally shared set of activities marked the "disintegration" of that community, which potentially reemerges the following year. This view implicitly abets the concept of culture as shared patterns of purposive activities.

By organizing this ethnography in terms of seasonal activities, I am able to descriptively analyze the differential effects of agents of change seasonally. The village is composed of individuals, a "cast of characters," who are continually adapting to changing personal, social and environmental conditions. Population increase and concomitant land scarcity, the growing incursions and effectiveness of national government institutions are the two most pervasive and obvious agents of change which affect the villagers.

Each chapter presents a normative description of sets of traditional tasks associated with each season, thereafter individual variations on these normative models are examined. Types of disputes associated with each season are described with individual case studies presented in depth.

The organization of this ethnography complements the villagers' own perceptions of their life cycle and thus has the advantage of being a more "organic" or "natural" method of ethnographic exposition than those which slice culture up into its various component "systems."

I begin with a brief introduction to the village of Kotabowa. My choice of Kotabowa as a fieldwork site was guided by a stubborn adherence to a normative image of what a non-Western village should look like. Though accidental, I could not have chosen a more enjoyable and interesting place to live. This introduction is followed by a "cast of characters"—those people who are frequent protagonists in the subsequent chapters. The remainder of the chapters adhere to the various seasonal cycles. Though the cycles represent a calendrical year, the data is a composite of nearly three years of residence in the village, from June 1979 to February 1982.

THE VILLAGE

Selecting a Village

Upon arriving in Sri Lanka in June 1979, I was prepared and intended to do fieldwork in a Sinhalese village. Sri Lanka is a predominantly Sinhalese nation (67% of the population is Sinhalese Buddhist and another approximately 7% are Sinhalese Christians). The Sri Lankan literature, as a result, focuses predominantly on the Sinhalese culture, secondarily on the large Tamil population, comprising 20% of the nation's population. I knew little about and was not interested in studying a Muslim community.

My original focus of research was to study patterns of cooperation and conflict in the context of leisure activities. I intended to find a Sinhalese village large enough to have play fields, inter- or intra-community team competitions and interlocal festivals. Since I was not limited to any particular area, I bought a 1952 Java motorcycle and toured the country in search of "my" village. I had innumerable opportunities to meet locals due to the consistency with which my motorcycle broke down.

In my head, I had an image of what I thought a village ought to look like. Time passed; in my travels I failed to find a village remotely resembling the model I stubbornly held onto. The towns appeared too large, unmanageable, and also foreboding with their hustle and bustle. The villages, on the other hand, appeared too decentralized, each residence being separated by gardens and cultivation plots. It was discouraging to imagine walking miles daily to intrude on and interfere with people's chores.

I was fortunate to meet Professor Gananath Obeyesekere at the annual Kataragama festival in 1979. I told him of my problems in finding a village, which sounded ridiculous in a nation full of villages. The following day an informant told him of a "miniature" Kataragama festival that takes place in a village called Kotabowa. After the interview, Obeyesekere turned to me and said, "that's where you should go." He

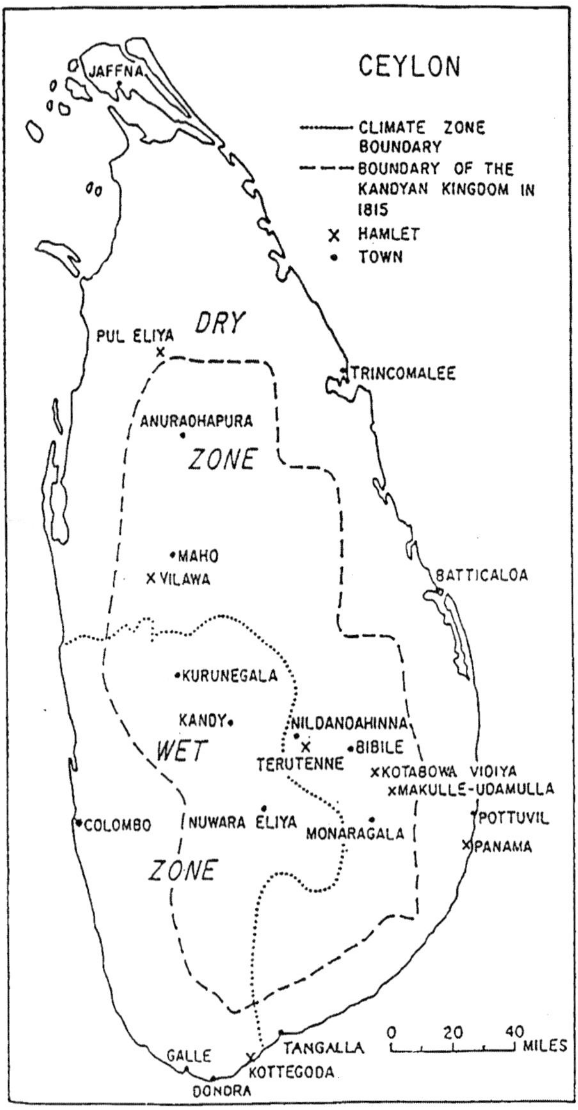

Figure 1. Sri Lanka

had no idea that Kotabowa was a Muslim village; the Buddhist "folk" temple located on its western boundary was removed from the village population.

Kotabowa is situated in the Uva Bintenne (or "basin"), Moneragela District of Sri Lanka. The nearest large town, Bibile, is approximately sixteen miles northwest of Kotabowa by road (see Map No. 2).

Bibile, a town of about 15,000, lies on an alluvial plain just below and east of the mountainous southwestern central region of Sri Lanka. Bibile, traditionally a rural, spartan town, was undergoing a period of transformation with gem shops opening up along its main street.

The road to Kotabowa is winding and poorly paved, six miles off the main highway connecting Bibile to the town of Moneragela. At the Kotabowa junction, where the pavement ended, was a cluster of shops and houses. Groups of villagers milled about and crowded around me. Fortunately, the *Grama Sevaka*, the government appointed "village headman", was present. The *Grama Sevaka*, commonly referred to and addressed as GS, was a Sinhalese man in his late forties who spoke English. I explained my objective and he was, and remained, a sympathetic and helpful supporter.

That afternoon he arranged a house for me to rent for seventy-five rupees per month (three U.S. dollars) and also a cook and general helper, Lafir. That afternoon, the GS and I ate lunch at a villager's house. Villagers, particularly children, looked on curiously through the door and windows. I left in the late afternoon, with everything arranged: I had "found" a village, obtained a house and servant, and was prepared to move in the next day.

Kotabowa fit my image of what a village should look like: the houses were close, there was a village "center", and I could easily travel along the dirt roads and footpaths visiting houses, cultivation fields and shops. The village possessed distinct geographical and socio-cultural boundaries that were lacking in the neighboring Sinhalese villages. The reasons for this, as I learned later, were the geo-social centrality of the mosque in Muslim communities and that historically villagers feared the possibility of communal violence, thus erecting their dwellings in proximity to one another for security. The cultivation fields

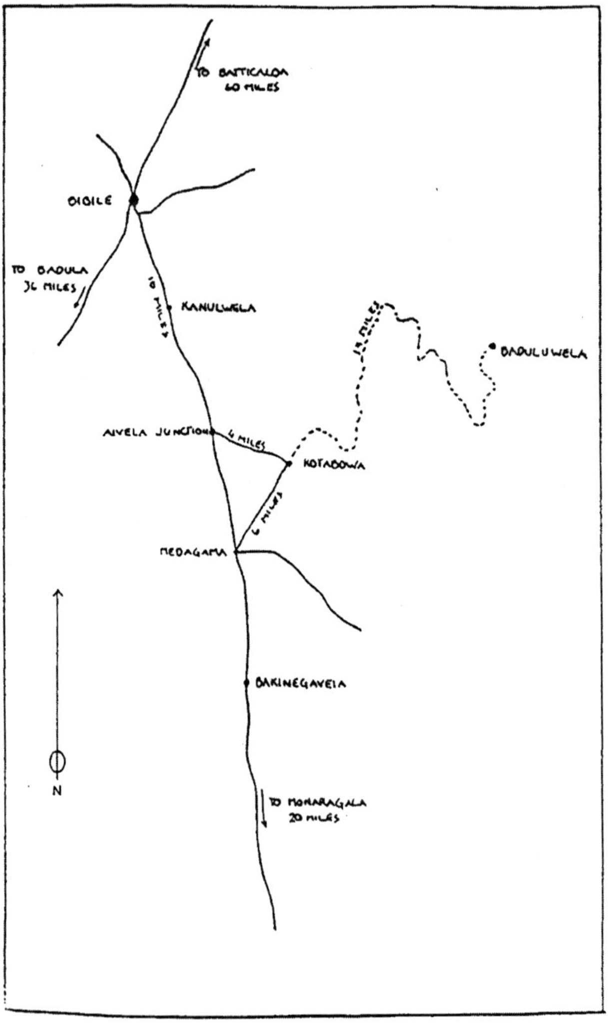

Figure 2. The Map of Kotobowa and Vicinity

encircling the village proper also served as a protective barrier deterring or forewarning villagers of possible communal attack. Kotabowa is an atypical village in the sense that the Muslim population of Sri Lanka tends to be concentrated along the coastal regions or in urban areas.

Origins of Kotabowa

The origins of Kotabowa are vague, clouded in myths and quasi-historical accounts. The village has a hyphenated name: Godigamuwa-Kotabowa. Kotabowa, literally translated as "short bow tree", refers to the 442 acres of *devale* (the Kataragama temple) lands. These lands historically "belong" to the *devale* and are managed by the government appointed administrator of the *devale*, called the *basnayaka* nilame. Villagers "lease" these lands for a traditionally nominal sum of one mat and five rupees paid annually. These villagers, in actuality, have permanent leases and consider these lands as their own.

Godigamuwa refers to all those lands which are not temple lands; these lands may be privately owned or government lands (colloquially referred to as "crown"). Godigamuwa is a Sinhalese name, referring to the Sinhalese hero, Gotimberre. Gotimberre was a short, extremely strong man who was said to have been one of the ten heroes who helped the Sinhalese-Buddhist King Dutugemunu defeat the Tamil-Hindu King Elara, in approximately 150 B.C. Many of the villages in the region have names referring to this historical battle, and it is probable that King Dutugemunu camped and rested in the area on his way to Anuradhapura where the battle was waged.

When and how Muslims first came to settle in Kotabowa remains conjectural. Arab traders were known to have visited Sri Lanka for commercial purposes in the second century B.C. An Arab traveler reported that "four Mussulman" were ministers for the Sri Lankan sovereign in 1154 A.D. (reported in *The Moorish Connection* 1976), suggesting the presence of a permanent Muslim population.

Historically, Sri Lankan Muslims were traders and merchants, the traders criss-crossing the country in *thavalams* (ox-cart caravans). The *Thavalam* route from the east-coast apparently passed through Kotabowa, where the traders rested and obtained such jungle resources as timber, *bidi* (cigarette) leaves, *nelli* (a fruit) and *areloo* (a dye and purgative). A few of these traders may have stayed in Kotabowa.

The origin legend of the *devale* also suggests the early presence of Muslims in the Kotabowa area. The legend tells of a king's son who had sculpted the face of the woman he intended to marry. The king displayed the sculpture and offered a reward to the person who found this girl. Two Muslim merchants came to Kotabowa where they saw a girl resembling the sculpture. As a reward, they were given *nindagam* (feudal entitlement) lands in Kotabowa. The head priest (*bethmay*) of the *devale* estimated that the temple was built in the late 1700's. Thus, if this estimate and story is accurate, Muslims settled in Kotabowa at the same time.

Another quasi-historical account refers to a Muslim physician being conferred with *nindagam* (feudal) lands in Godigamuwa as early as 1760 (see *The Moors of Sri Lanka* 1976:197–199). A few elder villagers related a similar account concerning a Muslim physician who, after curing the queen of dropsy, was given a Sinhalese bride and the *nindagam* lands of Godigamuwa.

Mr. Kotagama, an elderly Sinhalese man who had served as a feudal administrator of the Bible area, believed that the main influx of Muslims to Kotabowa occurred between 1810 and 1820 as a result of Sinhalese-Muslim tensions. During that time, according to Mr. Kotagama, the English appointed a Muslim as viceroy (*Mohandiram*) for the Moneragela Province. In 1815, with the fall of the mountain kingdom of Kandy, the British had taken the entire island under their rule. The Sinhalese were thus forced to drink a doubly bitter cup: the end of an independent Sinhalese nation and the installment of a Muslim viceroy. A rebellion broke out in the area and a Sinhalese officer, Kepitipola, was sent to squelch it. Kepitipola sympathized with the rebels and became their leader; he was said to have camped and discussed strategy in the Kotabowa *devale*. Kepitipola's forces were defeated and he went into hiding. A Muslim was said to have reported his hiding place to the British and he was subsequently hanged. Kepitipola became a Sinhalese hero and Muslims were blamed for his capture. Many Muslims, according to Mr. Kotagama, thought it safer to leave the neighboring town areas And relocate in the more remote area of Kotabowa.

Village Setting

The roughly triangular "central highlands" of Sri Lanka are circumscribed by plains of low relief, approximately 300 feet above sea level (Peiris 1977). Kotabowa lies approximately ten miles east of the base of this mountain chain. The temperature of Kotabowa has little seasonal and diurnal variation, ranging between 75 and 85 degrees Fahrenheit. In the absence of thermal variations, seasons are marked by variations in rainfall. Kotabowa lies in the transitional rain zone, between what are called the dry and wet zones. Rainfall is less predictable in the Uva Basin, where Kotabowa is located, than in other regions of Sri Lanka (Pieris 1977). The rainy period is between October and February, with monthly averages of approximately 20 inches. The heaviest rains generally fall between November and early January. Rainfall patterns are erratic, often coming in heavy short monsoon bursts followed by days without rain. The monsoon rains are often as destructive as droughts, flooding fields, drowning crops and breaking the patchwork of sidewalls separating paddy plots from one another.

The population of Kotabowa, as for the rest of Sri Lanka, has increased at an explosive rate. In 1971 the village population was 767, in 1981 it was 1100: an increase of 43.4%. This increase was due to a number of factors: (1) the crude death rate on the island has dropped from 21 per 1000 in 1943 to 7.5 per 1000 in 1970. On the other hand, the crude birth rate for the island has remained fairly steady through the 1900's (about 37.5 per 1000). These same trends are reflected in Kotabowa (though I lack accurate statistics for local births and death rates over a decade). (2) The primary reason for the population increase is the effectiveness of government programs to eradicate malaria and other epidemical diseases and the free government hospitals. There were two government hospitals within easy reach of the villagers: in Bibile and Medagama. (3) Since the 1970's there has been an influx of Sinhalese settlers to the Kotabowa area. These recent settlers were attracted by the availability of lands in the region. The population of Kotabowa is likely to continue to explode as in 1981, 55% of the population was fourteen years old or younger.

Kotabowa, as mentioned, lies on the western edge of the Nilgala jungle. Elephants, monkeys, wild boar, deer and an occasional leopard

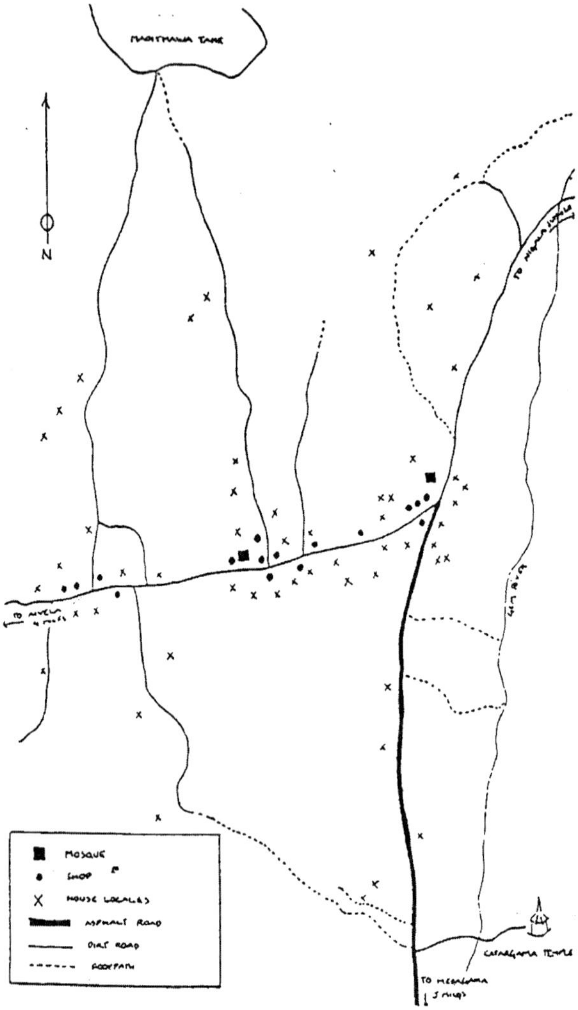

Figure 3. Kotobowa

inhabit the jungle and, except for leopards, these animals frequently destroy cultivated fields. Until 1976 there had been no bus service or paved road connecting Kotabowa to the wider world. The populations of the neighboring hamlets and villages are Sinhalese. As a result of this historical period of geographic and social isolation from other Muslim communities, the Muslims of Kotabowa had adopted many traits more characteristic of Sinhalese than Muslim communities.

The villagers speak a Tamil dialect, the lingua franca of Sri Lankan Muslims, which also includes a large number of Sinhalese words. Village males are equally conversant in Sinhalese and Tamil, while most of the women understand but are unable to speak Sinhalese.

Women move freely about the village without veils covering their faces. It is not uncommon to witness men and women disputing or conversing in public places. Women, however, will not visit shops simply to socialize like the men. Women labor in the fields and, if necessary, perform tasks that are normally the domain of men. In general, women had a freer rein in Kotabowa than in other Muslim communities I visited.

The folk beliefs and practices of the Muslims and Sinhalese of the area are similar. Buddhists charmers (*katadhis*), folk healers (*waede mahatteyas*), folk priests (*kapuralas*), and even Buddhist monks (*bhikkus*) were often enlisted for specific services by Muslim villagers. During the Kataragama festival season, it was not uncommon for villagers to, albeit surreptitiously, offer a vow to the gods. The license to shift freely from Islamic to Buddhist customs, beliefs and practices is becoming constrained as connections with the wider Muslim community are increasing.

A CAST OF CHARACTERS

In the following chapters a number of villagers are mentioned and discussed repeatedly. These profiles are meant to help the reader avoid the kind of confusion that can be caused by the introduction of numerous strange names. These profiles are brief schematic sketches, intended to serve as "aids".

1. **Assistant Government Agent**—usually referred to simply as AGA. He is the government officer in charge of the Medagama *pattu* (or division) in which Kotabowa is included. He is responsible for the bureaucratic administration of the division and the immediate supervisor of the *grama sevakas* for that division. All villagers' petitions for business, food stamps, land permits, etc., must be approved by him.

2. **Adam Marikar**—a sixty-five year old man and the ex-trustee of the mosque. The trustee is the designated leader of the administrative aspects of the mosque (i.e., organizing festivals, registering births and marriages and dowries proffered, and arbitrating over disputes that concern the mosque). *Marikar* is a title which refers to these mosque officials; the chief *marikar* being referred to as "trustee." Though he is no longer the trustee he serves as an "honorary" trustee and remains an active leader in mosque affairs. In a questionnaire he was selected most frequently as a village leader.

3. **Amina Umma**—a woman in her mid-twenties who was married to the son of the ex-village headman. She was from a town in the central highlands of Sri Lanka and had married against her will. A very despondent woman, she was openly critical of village ways and was the only villager that was consensually ostracized by both male and female villagers. She was a primary female informant.

4. **Farook**—a close friend of mine who also volunteered a great deal of information. He was in his late twenties and, like many younger adults, chafed under the economic limitations of village life. His friendship and cooperative efforts with Siddik are discussed in parts of this manuscript.

5. ***Grama Sevaka***—usually referred to as GS. The government appointed village headman. The problems of the GS, as a village outsider and Sinhalese Buddhist, as well as his problems with performing his duties and enforcing his authority are discussed throughout this manuscript. An intelligent and clever man, he was a close friend of mine as well as one of my primary informants. His knowledge of local and national level politics and acumen at deciphering individual strategies at both levels was remarkable.

6. **Hamsa**—a *marikar*, shopowner and trusted friend. He possessed a community reputation for honesty and, joined with his considerable business skills, ran one of the most successful shops in the village. During my three years in Kotabowa only Hamsa's and one other shop managed to stay open throughout.

8. **Hassan**, the Trustee—Hassan, in his late forties, was selected as the mosque Trustee, succeeding his elder brother, Mohideen, to the post. A relatively poor man, he was the undisputed leader of the mosque.

9. **Ibrahim Maulevi**—*Maulevi* is a Muslim title referring to Muslims who have been trained and graduated from an Islamic school. *Maulevis* can speak and understand religious Arabic, and are trained in the Koran and Islamic law. Ibrahim was in his early twenties and single. He was the "second" *Maulevi*, referred to by villagers as "Sinai Maulevi" (small *Maulevi*) as opposed to the chief *Maulevi*, Nauman. Ibrahim was the Islamic teacher for the village children. He was a devout and orthodox Muslim, who was perhaps the most respected person in the village. He was the village leader of the Jamaat Tablik, a national movement to return Muslims to the orthodox fold.

10. **Lafir**—Lafir was my servant; a young man who turned twenty during my stay. He was extremely loyal and an excellent informant.

11. ***Lebbe***—*Lebbe* is the title used to designate the mosque priest. It is a "folk" assignation, and is often incorporated in Muslim family names. Not all *Lebbes* are priests and not all priests are *Lebbes*. *Maulevis* may also serve as mosque priests and replace the *Lebbe*. However, in Sri Lanka most mosque priests are *lebbes*. *Lebbes* receive informal training, usually from their father or uncle; the *Lebbe* post is hereditary. As a rule, *Lebbes* can recite Arabic prayers but they, unlike

Maulevis, have no understanding of the words. *Lebbes* are paid a salary by the mosque. The *Lebbe*'s tasks include selecting the names for newborn infants, selecting propitious days for weddings, sowing and the like, and offering a variety of vows (to saints) for protection of property, health and prosperity. The *Lebbe*, in contrast to the *Maulevi*, may usefully be thought of as a folk priest whereas the *Maulevi* is (usually) a representative of Islamic orthodoxy.

11. **Latif**—the leader of the group of young adults I call the "young Turks." He was in his late twenties and was ostensibly the most economically upwardly mobile of villagers. He had obtained his wealth through shrewd business dealings and the luck of finding a valuable gem. In 1981, he had opened up the village bakery, obtained the contract for the village butcher stall, erected a new concrete three room building on the Kotabowa junction where he opened up a shop, was voted president of the Village Cooperative Society (a potentially lucrative position).

12. **Member of Parliament**—usually referred to as MP. The MP may usefully be thought of as a feudal sovereign; he is commonly spoken of as a "mini-king." The MP, if he so desired, could exercise his authority over any public agency (including the AGA and police department) in his electorate. The MP is in charge of the allocation of public sector jobs and is the main channel whereby people receive services from government agencies. He may allocate Crown (government) lands, grant crop subsidies and obtain transfers for public servants, either for good or ill. The MP possesses near total political control over his electoral district and is capable of countermanding the decisions of the AGA and other government officers. Village political brokers wield a lot of indirect power through their connection with the MP.

13. **Mohideen**—a political leader in the village. He was an ex-trustee, replaced by his younger brother, and was an assistant cultivation officer in charge of the regulation of irrigation water to paddy fields. Mohideen had also served as the village representative to the Village Council (disbanded in 1978). Allied with the UNP party he served as a political broker and obtained a number of lucrative building contracts. Mohideen, in his fifties, had lost respect in the village because of his frequent drinking sprees and subsequent abusive behavior.

14. **Muthulingam**—my interpreter and close friend. A Tamil who had been raised on tea estates; he was a poor man who earned his living repairing sewing machines, hence the nickname "Singer." Mr. Muthulingam spoke fluent English and Sinhalese, as well as his native Tamil. His relative poverty was, for me, a boon, since he was accustomed to village life and neither considered himself nor was considered to be "superior" to villagers. Muthulingam also possessed considerable social skills and was adept at eliciting information in very roundabout ways. As a favorite drinking companion of Mohideen, he was able to elicit information that I would otherwise not be able to obtain.

15. **Mynah**—a nickname for a female villager reputed for her verbosity. She was married, with four children and in her mid-twenties. One of my primary female informants.

16. **Nauman Maulevi**—the chief *maùlevi* in Kotabowa and also one of the two permanent schoolteachers. He was married to Mohideen's daughter and through his link with Mohideen was also one of the village UNP leaders. He also served as president of one of the two Rural Development Societies in the village. A very influential villager who, with the Trustee, served as the religious leader of the village. Nauman had earned the criticism of some detractors in the village who did not think a religious leader should be as politically and economically active as Nauman was.

17. **Omar**—a *Marikar* and son of Adam Marikar. In his late thirties; he was very active in village affairs, particularly those involving the mosque.

18. **Pitchai**—along with Mohideen, he was the UNP leader of the village and served as a political broker. He was closely aligned with Mohideen. Pitchai was in his early forties and is position as a village leader was distinctly on the rise while Mohideen's may be said to be on the decline. He was an active spokesman for the village in attempting to elicit programs for the improvement of the village. He was the president of the second Rural Development Society, an ex-*Marikar*, assistant cultivation officer, and the only villager active as a middleman between villagers and urban merchants. He earned much of his income by buying *chena* crops, bananas, timber, *bidi* leaves and other resources

from rural areas and selling them to merchants who visited local fairs. Pitchai would be my choice for the actual and most effective leader in the village.

19. **Salaam**—the principal of the village school. He had been transferred to Kotabowa in 1977, possibly because he was an ardent supporter of the SLFP. In his late thirties, he spoke a modicum of English and served as a field assistant and friend to the author. The maps and village kinship chart were drawn by him.

20. **Suwanda**—the Sinhalese charmer (*katadhi*) enlisted by villagers to treat a variety of illnesses and misfortunes. Treatment consisted of reciting *mantrams* (magico-religious verses) to drive away *yakkus* (demons) and providing herbal remedies.

21. **Waede Mahatteya**—a Muslim man in his mid-sixties. He was the village snake doctor and also cured other types of ailments. He had an extensive knowledge of village and religious lore, herbal medicines and sundry kinds of folk practices and beliefs; he was a gold mine of information. *Waede Mahatteya* is a Sinhalese term used to refer to folk doctors and the name he was commonly referred to and addressed by.

CHENA LANDS

Introduction: Old and New Strategies

For the Muslim villagers of Kotabowa, the majority of whom work paddy fields, *chena* crops serve as a supplementary source of food and income prior to the paddy harvest. A *chena* is a piece of land which is left to lie fallow for a period of years, ideally five, and then prepared and cultivated for one year. Traditionally, *chena* lands are temporary, undeeded lands located on high, usually sloping ground not suited for paddy cultivation. The two main crops are maize, *Zea mays*, (called Indian corn by locals) and finger millet, *Eleusine coracana* (called *kurakkan*). Secondary crops include manioc, sweet potatoes, beans and varieties of pumpkin. The aforementioned crops are said to require less rainwater than paddy and are harvested before the paddy crop.

It was nearly impossible to obtain accurate data on the total or average acreage of *chena* lands in Kotabowa. There are two reasons for this: (1) *chena* lands are (by definition) cut from untended forest lands, usually not legally titled land; (2) the size of a *chena* plot depends on labor resources, time, and natural boundaries (steep slopes, crevasses, streams and trees). Villagers, when asked, estimated the size of their *chena* as being one, one and a half, or two acres.

Of the 203 Muslim families surveyed by the author in 1981, only eight did not work their own *chena* field; all of the thirty-three Sinhalese families surveyed worked a *chena* field. The fact that nearly all villagers cultivated a *chena* was not surprising. A survey of land acreage in the Kotabowa area showed that a total of 442 acres of temple (*devale*) highland, 500 acres of crown (government) highland, and 80 acres of private highland were all potentially available for *chena* cultivation (minus permanent dwellings, roads, rivers and tributaries). *Chena* fields could also be cultivated with little (and potentially no) capital outlay. Third, the Sinhalese were mostly recent settlers from neighboring villages where land was scarce and came to Kotabowa in order to set up permanent *chena* fields.

The traditional cycle of annually rotating three or more *chena* lands was gradually changing. Adam Marikar, a sixty-five-year-old man, noted that, "Traditionally you could work a *chena*, take the yield and leave it to mature, but now there are no available forest lands so you must collect the harvest and come back the next year."

The present danger with the traditional strategy of shifting cultivation is that someone will claim the abandoned fields for permanent occupation. Thus, a new strategy, operative for many villagers, was to claim a permanent *chena* field even though yields may diminish with annual cultivation. To lay claim to a *chena* field one must either put a fence around it (usually of branches roped together with bark), or build a permanent dwelling on the land. Permanent crops such as banana, coconut, orange and lime trees, and tubers such as sweet potato and manioc, are planted in these permanent *chenas*. Adam Marikar says of manioc, "(it is) ... a permanent crop which you can harvest forever. However, the first year you get big maniocs, the second year only half the size, and the third year only small roots. Thereafter you must dig up the land and you can cultivate again with no problem."

After staking claim to a permanent *chena* field, villagers must first obtain a letter of recommendation through the village headman (*Grama Sevaka*) or agricultural officer (*vel vidane*). The recommendation must then be approved by the Assistant Government Agent (called the A.G.A., or D.R.O. for District Revenue Officer). Increasing population pressures, scarcity of level and easily accessible highlands plus the increasing effectiveness of government policies prohibiting the cutting of forest lands have compelled many families to build permanent boundaries around *chena* lands traditionally considered "free" and available. Most villagers still maintain the traditional strategy for selecting temporary *chena* lands. However, observation and data indicated that the mean fallow period was less than five years. Data for ten *chena* fields showed an average fallow period of 3.5 years. One informant noted that he had a two acre permanent *chena* field, working one acre one year, the other acre the next year. It is probable that in the future similar practices will predominate and the fallow period for *chena* fields will decrease.

Another innovative strategy, applied by those families who have the financial and human resources, is to claim a permanent *chena* field and work a temporary *chena* simultaneously. For example, "Foxer" ("Nariyar", nickname given by the villagers because this man once returned from a hunting expedition with a fox), worked two *chena* lands in 1981. On his permanent *chena* he grew manioc, bananas, coconuts, eggplant, mango, papaya, cowpeas and maize once every three years. On his temporary *chena* he cultivated millet, cowpeas and maize. The first *chena* was fenced; the second was not fenced and had been worked four years earlier. Neither of these lands were deeded. Foxer noted that, because of the influx of Sinhalese into the area, there are fewer *chena* lands available.

Another factor altering the traditional *chena* strategies is that in 1979 the Sri Lankan government passed a law prohibiting the clearing of jungle lands without a permit. While this law remained ineffective in remote areas, such as Kotabowa, it motivated villagers to apply for land deeds or long-term leases of government lands. In February, 1981, the last land *kacheri* was held in Kotabowa. Previously, land *kacheris* were held annually for the purpose of "regularizing", i.e., acknowledging and distributing land permits for government lands. Villagers were allowed to claim no more than two acres of lowland and one acre of highland and must pay a nominal fee of two to five rupees for such lands. The A.G.A., assisted by the *Grama Sevaka* and *vel vidane* of the village, listened to the various claims, asked if there were any objections, and, if there were none, registered the claim. Legally, the land is consigned on temporary ninety-nine year leases and must remain in the family, i.e., given to a son or daughter.

Traditionally, villagers did not need to "regularize" temporary *chena* lands. All villagers, according to Foxer, knew where everyone's *chena* lands were, and there were no problems unless someone intentionally encroached. Due to the effectiveness of implementing government policies and the presence of government agents in the village, there has been a concomitant shift from public recognition of non-titled 'historic' ownership of land to official deeds as legitimate proof of ownership. For example, Hakeem had been working his father's *chena* field when his *maama* (uncle) came to tell him to stop working since he (the *maama*) had a permit. Hakeem's *maama* threatened to go to the police if Hakeem did not leave the land immediately. According to Hakeem, his father had the historical right to the property but the family was too poor and had not bothered to obtain a permit: "If the police come I will definitely have to give it back since we took no steps to apply for a permit. So, now, how am I going to work a *chena*?"

Another method used by villagers to obtain long-term permits for government highlands was by taking advantage of government schemes for encouraging villagers to grow cotton, coffee, sesame and other cash crops. For example, five villagers applied for cotton permits. All were given long-term leases, plus loans and instructions on how to grow cotton. The *vel vidane* was to check the villagers' progress. Japan Mudallali (*Mudallali* means merchant or businessman, and "Japan" is his nickname in reference to his enterprising nature) procured five acres off the Nilgala-Medagama road (see Map 3). The loan money was used for immediate needs, though he did grow cotton and sesame on this land. Japan Mudallali said that, from one seeding of cotton, he can obtain a harvest annually for three years. He noted that the first harvest would bring an income of approximately 1500 rupees, and he estimated an expenditure of 2000 rupees. However, aside from cost and income, Japan Mudallali explained that the work was too much trouble for him to do again. His interest was to satisfy the government requirements and then cultivate permanent *chena* crops on the land.

Beside the 500 acres of government highlands, there are also 442 acres of temple (*devale*) highlands in the Kotabowa region. *Devale* lands are usually obtained by contacting the *basnayaka*, the administrator of *devale* lands and *devale* functions. The *bethmay*, the head priest of the temple, may also be contacted. The traditional payment for permanent habitation of *devale* land is five rupees and a mat annually. For the last twenty years, this task had been delegated to the village *waede mahatteya* (snake doctor), Hassaner Lebbe. Temporary *chena* lands were cleared without obtaining permission and without charge. Sinhalese settlers and Muslim villagers contacted either the *bethmay* or *basnayaka* to obtain leases for *devale* lands. Payment for such land was negotiable and seemed to depend on the whim of the *basnayaka* or *bethmay*, as well as the influence of the settlers. For example, one low-caste family (pottery caste) from a distant area paid 1500 rupees for fifteen acres of permanent *chena* land while a high-caste farmer, the local bus driver, received three acres of permanent *chena* land without charge.

I estimated that, out of a total of 442 acres of *devale* highland, 500 acres of government highland, and 80 acres of private highland, 224 acres were officially claimed by deed or lease permit. After eliminating private lands, there remain unclaimed 778 acres of government and *devale* highland. If lands not amenable to cultivation of any kind are taken into account, there remain approximately 500 acres of potential *chena* land: enough for each of the 233 Sinhalese and Muslim families living in the Kotabowa region to clear one acre every two years. Of the thirty-three Sinhalese families, only one (to my knowledge) cultivated a temporary *chena*.

The above data and discussion demonstrate that in terms of the old strategy there is a scarcity of temporary *chena* lands. Villagers were in the process of shifting their strategy towards claiming permanent *chena* lands, and consequently emphasizing permanent or semi-permanent crops. It should be noted that the vast Nilgala forest lies beyond the boundaries of Kotabowa, and excessive competition for land would compel the villagers to clear this land, despite government prohibitions and danger from wild animals.

Selection of a *chena* field

Selection of a *chena* field is as much a group decision as an individual one. Since *chenas* are cleared on untended forest lands it is important for one's protection, as well as for that of the *chena* crops, to clear a *chena* field adjacent to other fields. One man said, "the clearing of a *chena* field must be done at about the same time by everyone for protection from wild animals and thieves. If you only have one solitary *chena* field, then you must keep an eye on it at all times. Not only will people know when the field is not being watched, but all of the wild animals in the area will concentrate on that field." Birds, monkeys, wild pigs, elephants and stray cattle can quickly destroy a *chena* field.

There were approximately eight large *chena* tracts in and around Kotabowa. Such tracts are selected for their accessibility by footpath or road and their proximity to the village. Two such tracts lie on either side of the Nilgala road, just past the main junction (see Map 3). In 1981, eighteen families cleared plots on the south side of the road, and twenty-five families cleared plots on the north side of the road. Most of these plots were between one and two acres in size, and all but one family was related to one or more families already working *chena* plots on that tract. An advantage of *chena* fields on the same tract with close kin is that close kin can easily be enlisted for *atam waede*, an important system of reciprocal labor exchange. Two additional advantages for families working adjacent *chena* fields on one tract are that relatives serve as potential allies inhibiting others from working *chena* lands during fallow periods, and as a means to regularize the fallow and cultivation cycles for a piece of land.

The types of kin relations between families that work *chena* fields on the same tract does not appear arbitrary. Table 1 below refers to the relationships between families occupying a single shared *chena* tract.

TABLE 1. Kinship Relations Between Chena Cultivators

BRO-SI	FA-DA	BRO-BRO	MO-SO	FA-SO	NON-KIN
7	3	3	1	1	3

total = 18

Since all Kotabowan Muslims are, however remotely, related to one another, the above dyadic links represent the most proximate kinship connections. The predominance of brother-sister and father-daughter links over other possibilities reflects the dowry-cross-cousin marriage preference system operative in Kotabowa (discussed in more detail in the marriage chapter).

Newly married couples without dowry *chena* lands and other families without "historical" claims to *chena* lands must find their own *chenas* each year, if they intend to work a *chena*. The most important factor, again, is proximity. Lands behind or near the permanent domicile or lands adjacent to large *chena* tracts are cleared for cultivation. It is important that the scrub, or forest growths, on the land be at least five feet in height, or, if not, that there be an abundance of decayed leaves on the ground. Large trees were also undesirable on *chena* lands since they obstruct sunlight. It was preferable, but not necessary, for the land to be relatively level. Of necessity, many *chenas* were cultivated on the sides of mountains.

Time is also an important factor in selecting a *chena* field. Chena fields must be prepared and sown before paddy cultivation starts, and before the heavy rains of the monsoon season begin. Jungle lands are cleared, and the cut vegetation must be dried for a few days in order to be burned. Rains will prevent the cut vegetation from burning and possibly keep the family from sowing the entire field. The ash of the burned vegetation serves as a fertilizer and insecticide for the crops; without this layer of ash, yields are small. Finally, if *chena* fields are cleared too late, labor otherwise needed for paddy cultivation will be diverted from *chena* work. Villagers select and prepare their *chena* fields between August and September; some tardy villagers delay till early October.

Preparation of a Chena Field

To prepare a *chena* field the lands must be cleared and the vegetation burned, the ashes spread, the field weeded, tilled and the seeds sown. Aside from the actual preparation, a fence should be built and a temporary tree or ground hut erected. A network of lines with cans attached is set up throughout the field; when pulled it makes a rattling sound which scares away birds and wild animals. Shelters, particularly on temporary *chena* lands, are makeshift affairs: branches cut from small trees provide the frame and bark the rope; wide *thallappa* (palm-like) leaves are used for the roof and walls; rough hewn planks raised off the ground with poles serve as a bed platform; and three conical-shaped rocks support clay pots used for cooking.

Jungle lands are always cleared by males. A long-handled scythe swung from side to side, low to the ground, is used to clear the large scrub. On occasions, one man may clear an entire *chena* field. For example, Tahir, a twenty-four-year-old single male, cleared an entire one acre field on his own in 1981; he worked for eighteen days beginning at sunrise, resting at noon and returned to work in the afternoon. Tahir lived with his parents and seven siblings. His brothers were too young and his father too infirm to help him. A large man of sixty-five called Malleyar, "Mountain Man," cleared an acre of land on his own the same year.

Most *chena* lands are cleared by the immediate family and with *atam* (free reciprocal labor exchange) and/or wage labor. Weeding demands the most intensive labor and is usually done by women and adolescents. Women and young adolescents line up side by side and use *mammoties* (wide-bladed hoes) to chop the weeds with quick up-and-down strokes. Holes approximately eight inches apart are dug with sharpened sticks and maize seeds are placed inside and covered with earth. After the maize seedlings break the earth, *kurakkan* (finger millet) is broadcast over the field.

One man of seventy-five pithily explained the sequence of preparing and sowing a *chena* field as follows: "If you begin too early, before the rains, then the seeds will die or you will get weeds and will have to turn them up again, doubling the work. If you wait too long you can't burn the vegetation; you will have to wait for a period of sunshine. After burning you weed and then sow the seed. For Indian corn you have to dig small holes eight inches apart and put two seeds in each hole, if one seed is bad the other will germinate. Sometimes the holes may be attacked by white ants. If the plant is healthy it will grow six to eight feet in height. On one acre you can plant about 500 Indian corn seeds which may give you a harvest of thirty to forty bushels. Between the corn you broadcast *kurakkan* and cover the seeds lightly; *kurakkan* grows up to two and a half feet. With an exceptional crop you may harvest 100 bushels. If the ground is bad [not fertile] the yield will be badly affected. Neither corn nor *kurakkan* require much water, and no manure or insecticide is used. Once that is over, you can broadcast some *gingelly* [sesame seed] which grows to three feet, and for an acre you can harvest forty to fifty bushels."

The above is a good overall description of the factors which are considered in preparing and sowing a *chena* field.

A major problem in preparing a *chena* field was finding an adequate labor force at minimum cost. Villagers have little income to spend, if any, for hiring laborers. Thus, most workers are enlisted by *atam* work. The problem with *atam* work is that equivalent labor must be exchanged.

Hameed, for example, reported that he had enlisted twenty-five workers on *atam* to clear and prepare his one and a half-acre *chena* field. Most of these workers were women, and he sent his wife and children to their fields to repay the *atam* work, reserving his own energies for other business, specifically for paddy cultivation. In 1981 wages for hiring a woman was five rupees per day (for men seven rupees per day), plus tea, betel chew and some foodstuffs. After the initial clearing of the field, the rest of the clearing and weeding is primarily done by women for three reasons: (1) weeding is not as physically demanding as work on the paddy fields; (2) wages for women are lower than for men; (3) exchanging female labor for *atam* work frees the men for other activities.

Table 2 below lists the acreage, the number of laborers enlisted on either *atam* or wage, and the crops grown for twenty-eight *chenas* on one tract. The list is intended to demonstrate the importance of *atam* work in relation to wage labor as well as the predominance of Indian corn (I.C.) and *kurakkan* (K) over other cultivated crops.

The importance of the *atam* labor exchange system for recruiting workers to help clear *chena* lands is highlighted by these statistics. The *atam* system is particularly important in villages such as Kotabowa where most villagers do not have the financial resources to hire laborers. The number of wage workers relative to *atam* laborers is compiled in Table 3 below.

Thus, 18 of 26, or 69% of the families, relied exclusively on *atam* work in preparing their *chena* fields. 22 of 26, or 85%, relied on *atam* labor exclusively and/or in conjunction with wage labor. Only 3 of 26, or 12%, relied exclusively on wage labor. It was only the relatively wealthy in the village who could afford to rely exclusively on hired labor.

Atam exchanges of labor are usually, but not necessarily, between close relations. This is correlated with the fact that close family

TABLE 2. Acreage, Type of Labor, and Variety of Crops Sown on *Chena* Lands

Field #	Acreage	*Atam*	Wage	Variety of Crops
1	2	yes	yes	IC, K, manioc
2	2	yes	yes	IC, K, cowpea, coconut
3	1	yes	no	IC, K, manioc, banana
4	3	yes	no	IC, K, long bean, banana
5	1	NO DATA		IC, K, cowpea
6	2	yes	no	IC
7	1	NO DATA		IC, cowpea, long bean
8	1.5	yes	no	IC, cowpea
9	1	yes	no	IC, K
10	1	yes	no	IC, K
11	.5	NO DATA		IC, K
12	1.5	no	yes	IC, K, pumpkin, cucumber
13	2	yes	yes	IC, K, long bean, cowpea
14	1.5	yes	no	IC, K, long bean, manioc, banana, cowpea, pumpkin
15	1	yes	no	IC, K, manioc
16	1.5	yes	no	IC, K, manioc, cowpea, bean
17	.75	yes	no	IC, K, cowpea, bean
18	1.5	yes	no	IC, K, manioc, pumpkin, cucumber
19	1.5	no	yes	IC, K, pumpkin, cucumber, banana, paddy

Table 2. *(continued)*

Field #	Acreage	*Atam*	Wage	Variety of Crops
20	1	no laborers engaged		IC, K
21	1	yes	no	IC, K, long bean, paddy
22	2	yes	no	IC, K, sesame, cowpea
23	2	yes	no	IC, K, pumpkin
24	1.5	yes	no	IC, sesame
25	2	yes	no	IC, K, sugar cane (100 plants)
26	1	no	yes	IC, K, cucumber, sesame
27	1	yes	yes	IC, K, beans
28	1	NO DATA		IC, K

TABLE 3. Wage Labor Relative to *Atam* Labor

		WAGE LABOR		
		yes	no	
***ATAM* LABOR**	yes	4	18	22
	no	3	1	4
		7	19	26

members tend to choose *chena* fields in proximity to one another. Kinship ties are important since *atam* contracts are implicit and must be reliably maintained from year to year. Friendships may end, *chena* fields may change annually, but kinship bonds remain permanent.

Tending and Guarding Chena Crops

Chena crops are harvested three to four months after sowing. During this time they must be carefully guarded from wild animals, stray cattle and thieves. Since the men are busy with the clearing and preparation of their paddy fields, their children, wives or parents (usually mothers) are left to watch the fields and sleep in thatched huts temporarily erected for this purpose. Women are seldom left alone; in particular, mature single girls are kept under close supervision by their mothers to guard against possible liaisons with boys. If the *chena* field is distant from their permanent housing, many families board up or lock their permanent houses and move into the *chena* huts, returning only for provisions.

Men cannot be relied upon to guard the *chena* fields. After the *chena* crops are sown, the energies of the males are concentrated on their paddy fields. Expenses for paddy cultivation are high, and most of the adult, male villagers are busy seeking loans, pawning jewelry, and engaging in petty enterprises to meet expenses for preparing paddy fields and acquiring seed.

During both day and night one can hear shouting and the clanging on cans, bells and other contraptions to frighten wild animals. Men carry old rifles to the *chena* huts at night for protection against elephants, and boys are armed with slingshots to ward off monkeys and birds.

Chena crops begin to ripen around December. Ears of corn are collected whenever someone is hungry. They are sometimes eaten raw but more often they are roasted or boiled in water. Women are recruited, usually on *atam* work, to harvest the Indian corn, *kurakkan* and long bean. These crops are laid out in the sun to dry, whereas the corn is dried in bundles suspended over the fireplace—the kernels to be pounded into flour later on. *Kurakkan* is dried, collected in gunny sacks and ground when needed. Tubers, beans, and other vegetable crops are also harvested by women as they ripen. Manioc, pumpkin, okra and sweet potato cannot be kept long after picking, so what cannot be eaten is given to relatives or sold in local shops. Most of the Indian corn, *kurakkan* and bean harvest is stored or eaten, the remainder is sold. These grains are not sold immediately, but in portions whenever the family needs money. Average yields for an acre range from ten to fifteen bushels for Indian corn and ten to twelve bushels for *kurakkan*. It is difficult to obtain accurate estimates since many ears of corn are plucked for immediate consumption, so the final harvest does not reflect the total yield. Few vegetable crops are grown on *chenas* in Kotabowa because *chena* crops are not cash crops, but primarily for family consumption. Vegetables cannot be stored and they are more susceptible to destruction by wild animals or insects. From December until March *chena* crops are the staple ingredients of the villager's diet. A typical morning meal consists of two ears of corn and tea. When the corn is pounded and ground to flour, *rotis* (like tortillas) are made and eaten with bananas or *sambal* (grated coconut meat mixed with chili powder). For lunch, the main meal, usually consists of *thallappa* (*kurakkan* boiled into huge, pasty doughs). Small pieces of *thallappa* are pulled from the dough, rolled into a ball, dipped into a meat or dry fish gravy and swallowed; they are difficult to chew. The purpose is to fill the stomach rather than to eat something tasty. At night ears of corn are usually roasted or boiled, the kernels flicked off with the fingers and eaten. After the *chena* harvest the crops are bundled and brought back to the family's permanent home.

Disputes During the *Chena* Season

The three most common types of disputes involve matters of theft, stray cattle destroying crops, and land. Another problem is that women have more freedom during the *chena* season, which gives men more opportunities to establish clandestine love affairs with both single and married women. Below each of the three kinds of conflict categories shall be discussed in turn.

(1) Land Disputes

In 1980, the village *Grama Sevaka* (government appointed headman), reported that there were approximately ten disputes in which more than one party claimed possession of a permit for one *chena* land. A particularly involved case concerned three parties, each with land permits for the same piece of crown land. Tadiyar was given *chena* land on dowry by his father-in-law. In September of 1980, Tadiyar complained to the *Grama Sevaka* that a man named Haniffa (no relation) was clearing this particular piece of land for *chena* cultivation. Hadji produced a land permit which he claimed was for that piece of land. Upon visiting the area, the *Grama Sevaka* found that approximately a quarter of an acre had been cleared by Haniffa. The *Grama Sevaka* told Haniffa that no one has the permission to clear land without a permit and told him to leave. Later, Tadiyar returned to the *Grama Sevaka* to inform him that another man, Abdul Azees, was clearing the property. The *Grama Sevaka* proceeded to contact Abdul, who said that his mother had a permit for the land, which he promptly presented. Thereafter, Haniffa went to the *Grama Sevaka* and showed him a permit for the same land. As the *Grama Sevaka* was unable to verify which permit actually applied to that piece of land, none of the three were permitted to clear it. He recommended that any of the three contact the A.G.A. (Assistant Government Agent) to verify his permit. None of the three did this. Eventually, Abdul and Haniffa reached an agreement and both of them worked a portion of the *chena* land. Tadiyar complained and the matter was reported to the A.G.A.. In the meantime, the former two had continued to work, sow and eventually harvest their crops from that acre of land. The *Grama Sevaka* noted that people always show him land permits; the problem is that land permits do not delimit boundaries, only lot numbers. The surveyor, stationed thirty miles away in Moneragela, must be contacted to verify the actual boundaries. It may take two or three years for the surveyor to come to Kotabowa, and even after his visit there is little to inhibit other parties in following years from clearing the same untended parcel.

Pitchai was involved in a *chena* dispute with a Sinhalese man, Premaratne, in 1981. According to Premaratne, he and his family had moved to the area in 1979 and cleared a two acre *chena* field adjacent to Pitchai's land. Pitchai wanted to extend his two acres and had begun to erect a fence on what Premaratne claimed as his own property. Pitchai went to the police station in Bibile and made an entry against

Premaratne. Approximately one week later, a police officer arrived by bus. According to Premaratne, the policeman said that, unless the A.G.A. settles the matter, the land cannot be given to either party. Both parties were told to contact the *Grama Sevaka* who was to arbitrate the dispute. The *Grama Sevaka* visited the land, demarcated a boundary with the consent of both parties, and the case was decided in Pitchai's favor. Premaratne had agreed to the decision because he said he was not a trouble-maker and was afraid that Pitchai or other Muslims would claim all of his lands.

Another land dispute occurred in September, 1981 between Omar and Hakkim concerning land adjacent to the two-acre *chena* land mentioned above. Omar had obtained a land permit for two acres of crown land and, according to Hakkim, cleared three and a half acres. Hasseem complained to the *Grama Sevaka* that Omar had encroached on his crown land, and in any case, cleared more land than he had been allotted. The *Grama Sevaka* inquired into the dispute and Omar replied that half of the additionally cleared land was claimed by Noor Din (his sister-in-law's new husband) and the other half by Omar's brother-in-law. Omar explained that he was clearing this land on behalf of these two parties. The *Grama Sevaka* agreed with Hakkim's claim and ordered Omar to vacate the land.

Thereafter, the *Grama Sevaka* referred the case to the A.G.A.. Both parties were instructed to appear at the A.G.A.'s office, but neither did. Hakkim had apparently given up pursuing his claim and cleared another *chena* parcel. It was apparent that Omar did not feel threatened by or compelled to heed the *Grama Sevaka*'s directive. Omar was a very powerful man in the village and felt he could simply use "clout" to obtain this land.

The *Grama Sevaka*'s jurisdiction is limited. He has the authority to arrest villagers and to confer judgments, but in reality he is limited to referring cases or suggesting agreeable compromises. This particular *Grama Sevaka*, a Sinhalese, was stationed in Kotabowa for three years, from 1979 to 1982. He lived in a nearby village and traveled by bicycle or on foot to Kotabowa once or twice a week. The salary of a *Grama Sevaka* is meager, about seven hundred rupees net a month. He is the only government official who visits the village regularly. He must of necessity maintain amicable ties with most of the villagers. He is often the victim of threats; the previous *Grama Sevaka* having been clubbed over the head and hospitalized. The assailants were never identified. In light of this, the *Gram Sevaka* was very reluctant to take strict action against villagers.

A dispute over *chena* land between Sinhalese and Muslims concerned the right of the Sinhalese to settle in the Kotabowa region at all. In 1974, a group of four Sinhalese families, all of whom where related by blood or marriage, settled and cleared permanent *chenas* in the Kotabowa area. When they first arrived and cleared the land, Muslims (spearheaded by Pitchai) objected that the land was theirs by heritage, and filed a complaint with the A.G.A.. The Sinhalese had gone to the A.G.A. and said, "If you give this land to the Muslims, where are we to go? We are also Sri Lankans." The A.G.A. gave them permission to settle on the Crown land. A few years later, Pitchai once again told the Sinhalese that they had no right to settle on the land in question as it belonged to Muslims. The Sinhalese replied that it was too late in any event to move by that time, and that they had chosen land far off the road on the side of the mountain to avoid these types of disputes. Again the A.G.A, intervened, scolded Pitchai and the other Muslims and told the Sinhalese to continue cultivating. The problem remains touchy since fourteen additional Sinhalese families have settled in that region. The Muslims feared that, because the Sinhalese are the majority ethnic group in Sri Lanka (and more specifically in that area), they will, with the consent and encouragement of the government, continue to claim lands in the Kotabowa area. The Sinhalese now living in Kotabowa were poor, landless cultivators in their natal villages and moved to Kotabowa for the opportunity to settle down and cultivate permanent *chenas*. Both communities depend on arable land for their livelihood. With the pressures of an increasing population and stricter enforcement of government regulations, the problem is likely to be exacerbated unless alternative sources of stable income are developed.

(2) Stray Cattle Disputes

Below are listed a variety of disputes concerning the problem of stray cattle destroying crops. The conflict dialogues demonstrate the problem of obtaining compensation for damages already incurred; in many cases the victim feels justified in committing public acts to defame the character of his opponent. By venting anger in this way the victim obtains some measure of revenge.

A widowed woman woke one morning and saw much of her *chena* crop ruined. She walked out of the house and began shouting, "Since I am a widowed woman no one takes care to prevent their cattle from straying into my *chena* field!" As a crowd gathered, she insulted the husbands of the women present, warning that they too would someday be widowed and left without provisions. After her cursing subsided, the crowd dispersed; no accusations were made directly and no recompense offered.

In another dispute, Shaul Hameed had interrogated Ishmael as to why he had allowed his cattle to ruin Shaul Hameed's *chena* field. Ishmael cursed Shaul, and questioned the assumption that the cattle that had destroyed the crops were indeed his. He accused Shaul Hameed of collaring cattle off the road and then tying them to his fence. Shaul's son intervened, telling Ishmael to shut up and not to use foul language against his father. Ishmael attempted to strike Shaul Hameed's son, but Adam Marikar broke up the fight and asked Shaul if he was certain the cattle belonged to Ishmael. Shaul was uncertain, and thus the dispute ended.

When Omar had found Sa'id's cow and calf in his *chena* field, he managed to catch and tie up the calf in the damaged field. Sa'id and his younger brother scolded Omar, "What you have done is wrong. We are all going to die one day, so what will you gain by tying up my calf? Allah will definitely punish you." Omar replied, "I have explained to you (earlier) that your cow destroyed my *chena* crop, so don't make me lose my temper. I won't even mind raising my sarong (to fight) if need be. Everyone knows I don't involve myself in unnecessary affairs, but I won't let this matter drop...I am not afraid of you." Thereafter the agricultural officer was called and came to the scene to inspect the damage done by the cow. He ordered Sa'id to pay fifty rupees to Omar, who returned the calf.

As a final example, Abdul Hameed (Pitchai's brother) saw seven cattle in his *chena* field and managed to tie two of them up. He reported the matter to the agricultural officer who, with the aid of the *Grama Sevaka*, discovered that Jailany Bawa was the owner of the cattle. Jailany initially denied owning the cattle. Abdul Hameed requested two hundred rupees for damages, which Jailany Bawa refused to pay. They eventually reached a compromise of fifty rupees payment with the understanding that if a similar incident occurred again, Jailany Bawa would have to pay two hundred rupees in damages.

If stray cattle damage *chena* crops, compensation can only be guaranteed when the cattle are tied up within the field in question. The agricultural officer must be called in order to assess the damages and fine the guilty party. Even in such instances, the matter may be dropped if the agricultural officer is not in the village or nearby as it would be difficult to locate him. Compensation also depends on the ability of the guilty party to pay the fine. Two hundred rupees, even if a fair assessment, is usually understood to be an unrealistic figure which most villagers are unable and unwilling to pay, thus settlements average around fifty rupees. When the injured party cannot locate or catch the stray cattle, there is little that he or she can do but castigate the assumed guilty party.

*(3) Disputes Over Theft of **Chena** Crops*

Petty theft of *chena* crops constitute the most frequent source of argument during the *chena* season. The Sinhalese in the area have large permanent *chena* fields which do not lie adjacent to one another, except for those belonging to close kin; in which case the work and harvest are shared. For the Sinhalese, the problem of theft is less significant than for Muslims, who have mainly temporary, unfenced *chenas*, consisting of numerous fields located in large tracts. Conditions for theft are favorable: temporary *chenas* are not always watched, boundaries are difficult to discern at a distance, visitors and passersby frequently enter *chena* tracts and it is easy to hide among the tall corn stalks. Further, income and foodstuffs are low in the village during the period in which *chena* crops begin to ripen. Grudges held from previous years and poverty make theft easy to rationalize, and it is almost impossible to identify or catch culprits, even if they are observed. For these reasons incidents of theft are seldom satisfactorily arbitrated.

For the injured party, verbal indictment of the guilty party in public affords the sole means of immediate retribution.

Meeran, the only man with a driver's license in the village in 1981, was working in Medagama as a tractor driver. Although he was one of the few self-employed villagers, he did not have much land and was not considered wealthy by his neighbors. In 1981 Meeran and his wife, Mukuluth, cleared a *chena* field adjacent to his father-in-law's field in addition to growing some *chena* crops behind their house. One morning, Mukuluth noticed that six pumpkins were missing. The neighboring women suggested that the women who lived across the street had stolen them. This seemed plausible since the suspected women had poor reputations in the village. Mukuluth stood at the edge of her property, screaming accusations across the street. Using a great deal of profanity, she indicted the neighboring women, not only for stealing her pumpkins, but also for behaving in a lascivious fashion. Her condemnation ended with a curse of death to all who consumed her pumpkins. As a crowd gathered, this tirade increased in volume and profanity. The accused (a woman and her two daughters) defended themselves and tried to assault the aggressor's sister. The sister's husband promptly intervened and ended the dispute, instructing the crowd to disband. Although the argument subsided, intermittent quarrels continued between these two families. Meeran is not from Kotabowa, and his father-in-law is an old, sickly man with no sons. The family across the street consists of ten people, not to mention numerous relations in the vicinity. Mukuluth's tirade served, not only to vent her anger and thus shame these people publicly, but also as a gesture to signify that she was not defenseless.

The last example of theft is more complicated as it involves numerous ties both of kinship and business alliance. Zeera is Loose's daughter ("Loose," his village nickname, refers to the man's unkempt appearance and capricious temperament). She had noticed some ears of corn missing and went out into the street to scold Jainuldeen's wife. Jainuldeen is considered one of the wealthiest men in the village, he is uneducated, very taciturn and private and has little influence in village affairs. Jainuldeen exited his house and shouted, "I am not afraid of any of you. I have a rifle and I know how to use it so don't continue your scolding, you pariah scum." Loose stepped forward, removed his shirt and challenged Jainuldeen to a fistfight. Iqbal, Zeera's brother appeared, slapped her and dragged her from the scene saying, "Thanks to your foul mouth all this has happened." Loose turned and scolded his son, saying, "You should go and assault those fellows; not your own sister! You act like a woman!" A crowd gathered and Jainuldeen, remaining tactfully behind the fence bounding his yard compound, said, "We also have corn. There is no reason for my children to enter your *chena*." Mohammdu, Zeera's father-in-law, came to the scene shouting, "Come any of you and see the tracks from the *chena*; they lead directly to Jainuldeen's house." He then tried to get members of the crowd to come but no one bothered. Eventually the fight subsided; the following evening Iqbal apologized to Jainuldeen, who often lent Iqbal money for various business ventures.

Disputes such as those above occur with such frequency, exploding with quite eloquent rage and subsiding so quickly into the quicksands of history that they are perceived by the villagers as a scene in a "black comedy." Frequently when antagonists are raging over relatively minor incidents (e.g., the theft of a few ears of corn), villagers will rush to the scene, sit and hoot at the performers, laughing and applauding as if it were a stage play. However, if some insult refers coincidentally (or not) to one of the spectator's relations, almost as if a button is pushed anger will brim over into a stream of well-chosen words. Antagonists are aware that the culprit cannot be identified, and unless crops are destroyed or the verbal assault turns into a physical assault, no other recourse can be taken except publicly shaming the guilty party. The traditional arbitrator or headman, a native of the village, is now retired and has no authority. The *Grama Sevaka* is not always in the village and, as he is also a Sinhalese with no family ties in the village, he must be careful not to make enemies in the village. Villagers guard their reputation zealously, and it is a matter of pride if one has not been involved in any disputes. As Omar noted in the cattle dispute, "Everyone knows I don't involve myself in unnecessary affairs..."

Conclusion

Two points stand out in the above discussion: the increasing scarcity of *chena* (as well as other) lands and the increasing importance of government agents and laws in regulating village affairs. Both are generated from sources outside the village to which villagers must respond with new adaptive strategies. These new strategies are not being uniformly adopted by all villagers. In fact, these strategies remain tentative and experimental rather than routinized, acknowledged alternatives. Few villagers have permanent *chenas* and villagers who planned to cultivate permanent *chenas* often neglect them after the harvest has been collected. Scarcity of *chena* lands has compelled many families to return to their *chenas* within two to three years, rather than maintain the ideal five year rotation. The influx of Sinhalese settlers, combined with the burgeoning population of the village, is likely to increase competition and disputes over *chena* lands. As I previously noted, a census compiled by the author and assistant indicated a 43% increase in the population for Kotabowa over the decade, 1971–1981.

Government regulations prohibit the clearing of Crown land without a permit. While this regulation has not been effectively enforced, it is probable that it will be in the future. The clearing of *devale* land is also prohibited without first obtaining permission from the *basnayaka*. Enforcement of this policy by the *basnayaka* is more difficult since he has neither the time, inclination, nor backing of government agents such as the police or A.G.A..

Without fertilizer, lower yields can be expected on permanent *chenas* and/or *chenas* rotated less than every five years. Permanent crops can be cultivated, but grains such as maize and *kurakkan* have an advantage in that they can be stockpiled, whereas vegetable and tuber crops (e.g., manioc, sweet potato) ripen and spoil and are also more susceptible to attack by rodents and insects. The traditional equilibrium of much land/few people is out of balance and alternative sources of income such as cottage industries or larger industries in the area are nonexistent. For these reasons, illicit activities such as hunting, the felling of trees for timber, and *ganja* traffic have proliferated. Village estimates of the number of families trafficking in *ganja* ranged between seventy and ninety percent.

Conflicts over *chena* lands and the destruction of crops occur almost daily during the periods when *chena* lands are being cleared and crops begin to ripen. It was impossible to collect data on most of these disputes, but to my knowledge between 1979 and 1982 (covering three *chena* cycles) none of these conflicts erupted into physical violence or permanent cleavage between families. This is due to the fact that *chena* crops remain of secondary importance relative to paddy cultivation and also because *chena* land remains available. Conflicts over land are initially brought to the attention of either the *Grama Sevaka* or agricultural officer for arbitration. If they are unable to resolve the dispute, the A.G.A. or police may be contacted. The A.G.A. and police have jurisdiction over a large area, so by the time they look into these disputes the *chena* crops may already be harvested. Further, it is expensive and time-consuming to visit the A.G.A.'s office in Medagama or the police station in Bibile. Finally, even if the villagers have land permits, exact boundaries are impossible to discern, and a surveyor must be called to accurately evaluate the claims from either party. The A.G.A. is usually contacted over major land disputes, generally involving paddy land, and only once to my knowledge involving *chena* lands (which dealt with the right of Sinhalese to settle in Kotabowa).

Disputes over stray cattle, if the cattle are caught and tied on the *chena* land, are settled through the agricultural officer. Damage is assessed and the owner of the cattle fined. Fines are usually compromised, based on the cattle owner's ability to pay. When actual proof of culpability is absent, the injured party typically resorts to verbal abuse of the presumed guilty party.

Eighty-five percent of a survey sample of twenty-six families use *atam* work when clearing their *chena* fields. The true percentage is probably higher since families whose field was cleared with wage labor or alone could have neglected to mention some work done by *atam* out of pride, a prominent personality characteristic among Kotabowans. I resided in Kotabowa over three *chena* seasons (1979, 1980, 1981), during which time no disputes over failure to repay *atam* work were reported. This is not to preclude the existence of such disputes but rather that they were either resolved privately or occurred infrequently. As a mechanism for recruiting labor, *atam* work functions smoothly. *Atam* workers are recruited within the kin group or according to proximity, the latter being an important factor. However, close kin tend to select *chena* fields in proximity of one another, combining both variables.

This chapter has outlined some of the features and dynamics that constitute Kotabowa as a village; the importance of land, *chena* crops, large cooperative networks for obtaining labor and aid, adaptation to external pressures, methods of arbitration, shame as a punitive measure, and reciprocal labor exchange. The following chapter will describe and analyze the organizational features and dynamics of paddy cultivation.

THE PADDY SEASON

Introduction

There is no more beautiful sight, to a Kotabowan, than a dense sea of green paddy stalks beginning to turn golden and bend under the weight of thick bundles of ripening seed. Conversely, there is no uglier sight than to see a few thin, unhealthy patches of paddy shoots on a parched, cracked piece of earth. Though some fields may use irrigation water, no field in Kotabowa can rely solely on irrigation water for a successful harvest. The primary, *maditawa* tank, like the paddy fields is also dependent on rainwater rather than water channeled from rivers or streams. The Manik Ganga (Gem River), running at a lower elevation south of the village, flows west to east, into the large Senanayaka Samudra (reservoir) which is used to irrigate the vast tracts of paddy fields in the Ampari District, about forty miles east of Kotabowa.

A good rice yield depends, among other things, on a fine balance of rain and sunshine. Rains should be light and intermittent so as not to flood the fields or erode the topsoil. Infrequent rains, of course, cause the soil to crack and the stalks to wither and produce a low yield or possibly die. Kotabowa, as mentioned, lies in the transitional rain zone; rainfall is erratic and unpredictable. 1979 and 1980 were, by all accounts, dry seasons. Though I do not have rainfall averages for those two years, yield averages were estimated by the agricultural extension officer at 25 bushels per acre. In 1980, 35 acres of cultivated paddy fields were reported to have "died." The above yield average is substantially below a national average in 1976–77 (for the *Maha* season) of 52 bushels per acre. However, 1979–80 were said to be drought years, and villagers expected yields of 50 bushels per acre in good years. On prime lands, prepared with fertilizer, weedicide and pesticide, yields up to 100 bushels per acre were harvested on occasions.

Since Kotabowa is located in a dry zone and lacked a natural or man-made source of perennial water, villagers were only able to grow rice once annually. In Medagama and Bibile irrigation schemes made it possible for some farmers to grow rice in bi-annually, in both the *Maha* (high) and *Yala* (low) seasons.

Prior to the paddy season, villagers were anxiously occupied with collecting money to meet their paddy expenses. Villagers would have to buy paddy for sowing if none had been saved. In 1981 the price for a bushel of paddy seed was seventy rupees. A common means to obtain paddy seed for villagers short of cash was to promise to repay each bushel of seed borrowed with a bushel and half after the harvest. Jewelry and other family valuables were pawned with banks, shop-keepers or private moneylenders. A few villagers also earned profits lending money at extreme rates of interest (between twenty and thirty per cent per season). Cattle, water buffalo, goats and chickens were also sold to meet expenses. Parcels of paddy land were also mortgaged to meet expenses for the remaining fields.

Villagers measure paddy lands in two ways: by the number of bushels or by the number of paddy lands. It was usually estimated that five bushels sown was equivalent to one acre. Two bushels per acre sufficed if fields were to be transplanted.

Some of the important distinctions between *chena* and paddy lands are: (1) paddy lands are at a lower elevation and on more level ground than *chena* lands; (2) nearly all of the estimated 409 acres of paddy lands cultivated by villagers are consigned by deed or lease; (3) for all paddy lands, trellis structured troughs are cut in order to distribute water evenly throughout the plot; (4) whenever affordable, fertilizers, weedicide and pesticide are used by villagers for paddy cultivation; (5) paddy lands are cultivated annually.

In 1981, 28 households of 184 surveyed (15%) did not own a paddy field. Of those 28 households, 13 managed to obtain and cultivate a field by some other means. Though data is lacking, it is probable that the 15 remaining households without paddy lands were comprised of older couples whose property had already devolved to their children. In 1981, 91.85% of the households surveyed cultivated a paddy plot.

Between 1974 and 1977, the Maditawa reservoir had been built with government funds. This rural development project was intended to open up 75–80 acres of new lands for paddy cultivation.

The Maditawa reservoir was to be a great boon to the villagers by opening up a large tract of highland for paddy cultivation. The development of a large dependable water source with extensive irrigation channels was greeted enthusiastically and both Muslims and Sinhalese from adjacent village areas, who rushed to claim and asweddumize (i.e., prepare land for paddy cultivation) land near the reservoir. By 1981 over 300 acres of land had been cleared in *deniya*, the name for land in the reservoir area. This set up the dilemma of how an adequate supply of water was to be distributed over three hundred acres of paddy land when the capacity of the reservoir was intended to irrigate eighty acres. All villagers obviously wanted their water, particularly during the dry times. This irrigation scheme was objectively a success, more paddy lands had been opened up and as a result villagers grew more rice. Subjectively, however, it was a failure, since a volatile and near anarchic situation had been produced with villagers fighting each other for water. This situation shall be discussed in detail below, in the conflict section of this chapter.

The remainder of this chapter is organized as follows: (1) a discussion of paddy land ownership and alternative means for obtaining paddy lands; (2) a detailed account of the process of preparing a paddy field with an emphasis on the kinds of labor-exchange networks utilized by villagers and expenses involved; (3) a similar account on the process of harvesting the paddy also including the kinds of religious rituals associated with the harvest; (4) a description of the kinds of conflicts occurring during the paddy season followed with a detailed account of two such conflict cases.

Paddy Land Holdings in Kotabowa

Paddy is both a cash and household consumption crop. The first priority of all households is to store away enough paddy for home consumption for the year. One bushel of paddy contains between twelve and sixteen "measures" of paddy (a measure being equivalent to one kilogram). Villagers estimated that a family of four uses about one measure of rice daily. Thus, at minimum, approximately thirty bushels of paddy need to be stored to ensure an adequate supply of rice for one year. Ideally, most families aim to store a minimum of fifty bushels, leaving enough bushels for sowing the following year, for religious offerings and for emergencies. Therefore, during a good year, one acre of paddy land is a more or less accurate estimate of the minimum amount of paddy land a household needs to meet its lowest subsistence needs. Food and kerosene coupons, foodstuffs grown in *chenas* and household compounds, livestock, petty business enterprises, and temporary "coolie" work provides additional income and food resources to meet the household needs.

Figure 4 (see page 49) is a bar graph showing the paddy holdings (in bushels) of 184 households in Kotabowa. This graph does not include paddy lands obtained by other means such as temporary lease or mortgage.

Ninety-one, or nearly half, the households do not own enough paddy lands to meet this estimated minimum level for subsistence. In drought years even the 43 households with holdings between five and ten bushels will be hard put to meet their basic subsistence requirements. If we use paddy as a measure of economic security (that is the estimated minimum level villagers can reasonably expect to meet their basic subsistence needs during one year), 49.5% of the villagers are below this minimum line. When we include those families with land holdings between five and ten bushels, 72.8% of the villagers fall at the border or below this index of economic security. Aside from the alternative economic strategies and resources listed above, villagers will also try to secure paddy lands by alternative means.

Adee (sometimes written as *ande*) transactions are the most common method for acquiring temporary paddy lands. The most common kind of *adee* contract is to pay the owner of the paddy land the equivalent number of bushels sown after the paddy is harvested. For example, if five bushels are sown, the lessee will pay the land owner five bushels of paddy after the harvest. Equally acceptable is to pay the land owner in cash at the cost per bushel or in bushels of paddy at the time of the *adee* transaction. There are other variations of this *adee* contract-owner and lessee may often share the cost and expenses and yield of a field or the owner may provide all the capital and resources necessary for the preparation and harvest of the paddy field and the lessee will receive some agreed upon percentage of the yield. Close

FIGURE 1: PADDY HOLDINGS (BUSHELS) PER FAMILY

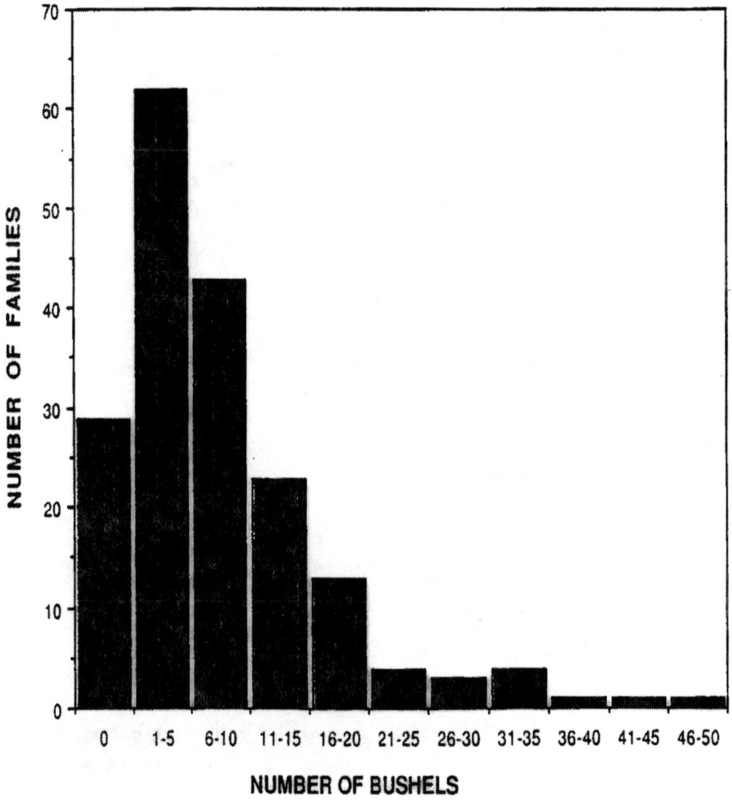

relations may also work the lands of elder relations or deserted or widowed women, giving these relations all or the majority of the harvest. For example, a man from Bakinigehavela (see vicinity map) returns annually to work his widowed sister's paddy field, giving her the entire yield. Another man works his parent's two bushels of paddy land at his own expense and gives them the yield.

In 1981, a survey of 184 households indicated that 45 (24.5%) obtained land through *adee*. Typically, most *adee* transactions are between relations. Table 4 below lists the relationship between the parties involved in these 45 *adee* transaction in 1981.

TABLE 4. Relations Between Parties In *Adee* Transactions

Land Owner	Receiver (Ego)	Cases
Parents	Son	4
Son	Father	2
Brother	Brother	2
MoSiSo	MoSiSo	1
Sister	Brother	5
WiFa	DaHu	7
WiBro	SiHu	6
WiSi	SiHu	4
MoBro	SiSo	1
Non-relation	n/a	13

Total Number of Cases = 45

Thirty-two (71.1%) of the *adee* transactions were between relations, 19 between affinal and 13 between consanguineal kin. Adee transactions where sisters are the land owners constitutes a special case, since in four of the five such transactions the sister gave land to a brother because there was no husband or elder son to work her lands. Excluding sister-brother *adee* transactions, 70.4% of *adee* transactions between relations were among affinal kin (19 of 27). The predominance of *adee* transactions between affines is, I think, a consequence of the dowry system.

Lands given by the dowry are always deeded to the wife (i.e., the daughter). If a family has a number of daughters they may not be able to provide equivalent shares of dowry lands for each daughter. In such cases, a man may regularly receive *adee* lands from his wife's parents or brothers.

Adee transactions were also motivated by economic needs and concerns. One Muslim villager, for example, offered to give four bushels (approximately one acre) of paddy lands on *adee* to a Sinhalese family. This contract was stipulated on the condition that both the Muslim and Sinhalese family shared equally in the labor, expenses and yield of this field. Aside from promoting good interethnic relations, this turned out to be a beneficial and satisfying arrangement for both parties. The Sinhalese family were recent settlers who possessed no paddy lands and the Muslim family owned numerous paddy fields but were short on cash and labor. Thus, the Muslim family was able to obtain reliable labor and necessary resources to successfully work all of their fields.

The most common economic motivation for giving lands on *adee* was when a family owned more than one paddy land but did not have the resources to cultivate both lands. In such instances, the family will usually give the poorer of these lands on *adee*. For example, one villager had cultivated a four-bushel plot for two successive years without receiving a sufficient yield to meet the costs of cultivating that field. He then offered this land on *adee* to another villager who had no paddy lands and could concentrate all his resources into this one field.

Villagers will also give their poorer lands on *adee* and obtain what they hope are more fertile lands in other *adee* transactions.

Adee transactions are always temporary, either for one or two seasons, with the land reverting back to the owner at the end of the stipulated time. Adee transactions are usually always notarized by the schoolmaster. The two parties agree on the contractual conditions and then, along with the notary, place their signatures on a stamp.

Adee transactions are a common method for obtaining paddy lands seasonally. It has the advantage that payments are made after the harvest at a small cost in the form of bushels of paddy. For the family giving land on *adee*, this is a method of ensuring a minimal yield on land that, in prior years, may have yielded less then the costs invested.

Giving land on *adee* also allows a household to concentrate its resources on those paddy lands expected to provide a high yield. Most importantly, the *adee* system serves as an opportunity for families without paddy lands to obtain such lands at a deferred cost.

Mortgaging paddy lands is a more complex process. In 1981, 7 families (3.8%) mortgaged paddy lands. Mortgaging lands differs in numerous ways from *adee* transactions: (1) usually land is only mortgaged as a result of dire economic circumstances; (2) the mortgagee pays the mortgagor immediately in cash; (3) the land owner may lose the deed to the land if he does not pay back the mortgagee within a stipulated time period. Mortgaged land is a contractual lien upon land coupled with the condition of defeasance on the payment of money within a specified period of time. If this payment is not paid the deed is then transferred to the mortgagee. The threat of loss of ownership makes this a desperate economic act.

Siddik explained to me that mortgage transactions should be between relations so that the mortgagee will be lenient and that the threat of losing the land deed is minimized for the mortgagor. Siddik also noted that should the mortgagor die, his immediate family may redeem the land. Further, Siddik explained, the mortgagee, over time, often begins to feel as if the mortgaged land is "his" even if the stipulated period of time to redeem the land has not yet expired.

In the event of a dispute, or should the mortgagor become greedy, he may destroy the deed in his possession, thus making it difficult for the original owner to reclaim his land. Although it is preferable to mortgage land between relations, villagers will usually go to whomever will give them the highest price or period to redeem the land. Only well-to-do villagers who already possess adequate paddy lands are in a position to buy lands on mortgage. The owner of the mortgaged land will annually receive the number of bushels sown at the time of the harvest from the mortgagor.

Preparation of Paddy Fields

The period from clearing a paddy field to sowing is one of frenzied and concerted activity, requiring intensive labor, the use of assorted types of equipment and animals, obtaining laborers, and a sizable capital outlay. The process of preparing and sowing a paddy field is a complex process consisting of coordinating a series of activities which must be coordinated with villagers who share adjacent paddy fields. The success of these activities depends not only on the farmer's resources and actions but on the weather. Too much or too little rain can ruin the best efforts. Villagers share an "ideal" model of how a paddy field should be prepared given enough financial, material and human resources. The first part of this section will describe this ideal model followed with examples of variations which are contingent on the individual's capacities to fit his activities with the ideal model. This comparative method was adopted to show that variations in the preparation process are not a result of "lack of knowledge" but of resources, and which kinds of variations are decided upon and how they are implemented.

The Ideal Model

Paddy fields are first cleaned: the fields are weeded, *bunds* (wide ridges which demarcate paddy fields and serves as footpaths) and sidewalls (thinner walls which segment one person's field into smaller sections) are also cleaned and/or erected. The initial weeding is usually done by women and children. This work must be done prior to the rains and, while requiring little capital outlay, involves a lot of labor. The weeding requires little capital because it is the only activity in the process of preparing a field that uses women and children as laborers.

Fields are divided into sub-plots by erecting sidewalls so that each sub-plot can be made level for water to be distributed evenly. V-shaped wedges of earth are cut from the sidewalls and used as gates for letting water in and out of each of these sub-plots.

With the first rains, water is left to stagnate in the field for five to ten days. Water may also be obtained from the irrigation channels. This is done in order to "muddy" the ground and to allow the weeds and grasses to decay. This is a simple but important procedure which requires no expense but is dependent on enough rain to fill the field.

While the water stagnates, farmers will shape and firm the sidewalls by digging up the muddy soil and spreading it along the sidewalls with their *mammoties* (wide-bladed hoes). This is a time-consuming task but usually requires no expense as villagers have five to ten days to complete it.

After the field is drained, teams consisting of two harnessed oxen or bulls are used to plow the fields. The plow is made of wood, usually with a sharp metal blade at the end to cut through the soil. It was estimated that four teams of oxen were required to plow a one acre field in one day. In 1981, the cost of a team of oxen and a "driver" was thirty-five rupees per day (twenty rupees for the team and fifteen for the driver). Wealthier villagers sometimes contracted their fields out for plowing at an estimated cost of one hundred fifty rupees per acre. Tractors were also contracted out on occasion at three hundred rupees per day. Only one villager to my knowledge contracted a tractor for plowing between 1979–1982. There were no tractors in Kotabowa or its immediate vicinity.

While many villagers own cattle, few own hefty bulls or oxen required for plowing. Villagers with oxen will usually exchange *atam* work with one another. Those without oxen were usually forced to hire such teams.

The first plowing is intended to loosen the soil and dig out the roots of the weeds and grasses. Teams of oxen follow one another with the plows furrowing rows ideally six inches (or so) apart. Water is then left to stagnate in the fields once more for up to ten days.

The field is plowed a second time and water is left to stagnate once more (but only for three to five days). A third plowing is optional.

A few days before the final sowing, water buffalo are used to trample through the field to break up dirt clots and to allow the water to seep deeper into the soil. Oxen may occasionally be used, but water buffalo are preferred as they are heavier and manage better in the mud. Water buffalo will cost twenty rupees per buffalo per day. The buffalo are usually not tied together and up to six will be set shoulder to shoulder and led back and forth through the field. The owner of the water buffalo will send a son to drive the buffalo and he will be paid fifteen rupees. This is an important preparational activity necessary for breaking up the clayish lumps of earth and is done by nearly all villagers. Since few villagers own water buffalo, most are forced to hire them.

A day or two after a field is trampled, it should be leveled and the finer clots of dirt are broken up with a rake-like tool attached to one team of oxen. The rake is wooden, about four feet in length and the driver stands on the frame of the rake for added weight. Only one rake is used since this is finer work and additional laborers are used to level and shape the field for final sowing. Approximately eight to ten laborers are required for this task for a four to five bushel field. The work is intensive since the field should be sown the following day.

A long level wooden plank is harnessed to a team of oxen and used to level the field. Laborers are used to cut the small water tributaries through each sub-plot. A main artery is cut, usually at a small angle, from one gate to the other, with arteries fanning out. As each sub-plot is completed paddy is broadcast over it. Again most villagers must hire a team of oxen and the wooden plank used to level the field for forty rupees (twenty for the oxen, five for the plank and fifteen for the driver). Eight to ten laborers are again required to dig the water channels and put the finishing touches on the field. A man who is reputed to be adept at broadcasting the paddy seeds must also be hired for fifteen rupees.

Prior to sowing, the paddy seeds are dampened and stored in a tightly wrapped gunny sack for three days to allow the seeds to sprout.

The first three days after sowing villagers do not want rain. The soil is already muddy and the seeds have not yet taken root. Heavy rains can ruin a field by causing the seeds to wash away and collect in the water channels or by the gate opening.

Ten days after sowing rains are desired and fields are filled with water which is immediately allowed to drain in order to clean the field of loose dirt.

When the first buds begin to appear on the paddy stalks weedicide and insecticide should be spread on the field. In 1981, the price of bottles of weedicide and pesticide were about eighty to ninety rupees,compared to twenty to thirty rupees the previous year. One bottle would suffice for a one acre field. A tank to spray these chemicals must also be rented at a cost of fifteen rupees per day.

On a dry day, about one month after sowing, fertilizer should be broadcast over a paddy field. Two 100 weight bags (224 pounds) should be used per acre. In 1981 each hundred weight bag cost one hundred and twenty rupees. Forty-five days after sowing fertilizer should be broadcast a second time over the field.

In 1981, fifteen villagers transplanted paddy. To transplant a field the same methods of preparation apply except that a nursery is planted in a section of the paddy field. For a one acre paddy field, two bushels of paddy are broadcast into the fenced off nursery plot. When the shoots in the nursery are about five inches tall they are transplanted. Both the nursery and the paddy field are filled with water so that the ground is muddy. Laborers are needed to pull the shoots from the nursery and bundle them. The hand-sized bundles are collected and transplanted in the larger paddy field. Water is drained from each sub-plot just prior to transplanting. The shoots are jabbed into the ground in a rapid-fire motion. A large number of laborers are required for transplanting. Of the two methods, broadcasting is the simplest and least expensive. Transplanting requires the same procedures and capital outlay as preparing a field for broadcasting plus the additional labor and expense involved in preparing a nursery and transplanting. The agricultural officer estimated that yields using the transplanting method will average eight-five bushels per acre. The paramount importance of a dependable water supply deters most villagers from transplanting their crop. Without a dependable source of water at the time of transplanting and the following days the tender roots of the paddy stalks will not take root.

The process of preparing a paddy field as described above involves a complex series of tasks which must be coordinated within a specified time schedule. The success of this process depends on obtaining labor, animals, and equipment and its success remains contingent on the unpredictability of the weather. The approximate expenses of preparing a one acre in 1981 paddy field if everything must be purchased is listed in Table 5 below:

Since most villagers do not have this kind of ready cash, even with *atam* arrangements, there are considerable variations of this ideal model.

Variations of the Ideal Model for Paddy Cultivation

There are probably as many variations on this model as villagers. Below six cases describing alternative strategies adopted by the villagers will be presented.

TABLE 5. Expenses for Preparing a Paddy Field

Activity or Items	Cost	
Five bushels of paddy	350	rupees
First plowing	140	"
Second plowing	140	"
Six water buffalo & driver	135	"
Rake w/ oxen and driver	40	"
Ten laborers	150	"
Wooden leveler w/ oxen and driver	40	"
Ten laborers	150	"
Weed and pesticides	160	"
Fertilizer (twice)	480	"
Tank rentals (for fertilizer and chemicals)	60	"
Total Expense =	1845	"

Case 1: Aliyar plowed his six bushel field with four teams of oxen. Two teams were obtained through *atam* and two were hired. The field took two days to complete and Aliyar paid one hundred rupees for the two teams plus supplying lunch, tea, cigarettes, *bidis*, and betel chew. He did not plow a second time because he said he had neither the cash nor the time. Aliyar owned a team of oxen and reciprocated the *atam* work. For the final preparation of the paddy field Aliyar hired a team of water buffalo, rake and leveling equipment and four laborers. He estimated his total costs at five hundred rupees, not including paddy seed.

Case 2: K. Salli was one of the wealthier villagers who owned five acres of paddy lands. He plowed his fields three times using his own teams of oxen. Ten laborers were hired for three days to plow the fields. K. Salli owned all the equipment and animals for the remainder of the preparation work but hired laborers for all the manual work. He and his three sons also worked. K. Salli estimated his expenses (not including weed and pesticide and fertilizer) at seven hundred and sixty rupees.

Case 3: K. Mohammed used five pairs of oxen, two his own and three received on *atam*, to plow his five acre paddy field. Four additional laborers were employed for wages totalling sixty rupees. He stagnated the water for ten days and followed this with a second plowing. This procedure was repeated a third time. Two brothers worked on *atam* during the entire preparation process, the remainder of the labor force was hired. Mohammed estimated his expenses at six hundred and sixty five rupees.

Case 4: Hasseem contracted out the first plowing of his three acre field for five hundred and twenty rupees, not including food and provisions. A subsequent plowing was contracted out for five hundred rupees. His father and three brothers provided water buffalo, equipment and *atam* work. Hasseem was employed outside the village as a bus driver and could not be present during the plowing of his field, therefore he contracted this work out. He estimated his total expenses at twelve hundred rupees.

Case 5: Hassan owned a six bushel field near the *maditawa* tank and used the transplant method because he was able to obtain water and regulate the water supply to his field. He sowed a nursery of two and a half bushels of paddy seed. He plowed his field using two teams of oxen and two brothers who worked on *atam* and two hired laborers. It took two days to complete the plowing at a cost of two hundred rupees. He did not plow his field a second time. The remainder of the work was done with the help of his brothers and other relations on *atam* as he had run out of money. He estimated his expenses for transplanting at one hundred and twenty rupees.

Case 6: Ishmael's three bushel paddy field was destroyed after the paddy seed was broadcast. Thereafter he purchased paddy shoots from a man in Kanulwela (a nearby village). He bought two bushels of paddy seedlings for one hundred rupees. Relatives and hired laborers were enlisted to replant the destroyed field. Fortunately, Ishmael was able to obtain enough water to prepare and transplant the paddy seedlings.

The work took two days and Ishmael estimated this additional expense at three hundred and fifty rupees.

Actual costs are far less then those detailed in the ideal model. Villagers rely heavily on *atam* arrangements for preparing their paddy fields. Villagers with cash and resources will plow their fields two to three times. One plowing sufficed for the majority of villagers. Water buffalo were not used by villagers who were short of funds. Villagers with no cash or equipment were often willing to substitute *atam* labor to level and rake their paddy fields. Fathers, sons and younger unmarried brothers provided a pool of free labor. The above examples indicate that in contrast to *chena* cultivation, some outlay of capital is necessary for the preparation of a paddy field: seed, laborers, equipment and animals are all essentials and potential sources of expense.

During the three months between sowing and harvesting, villagers will visit their paddy fields daily. Watch huts are erected in the middle of paddy fields and the household head sleeps there guarding the fields from animals. If the fields are located in *deniya* villagers will also be busily engaged in diverting water from the irrigation channels under the cover of the night.

By the end of December, all of the paddy fields in Kotabowa have been sown. In neighboring areas where paddy lands can depend on irrigated water, sowing may begin as late as January. Monsoon rains are the heaviest in December and January, averaging about twenty five inches per month (see Pieris 1979). Monsoon rains tend to be erratic with heavy outbursts of rain followed by days or weeks of no rain. These long dry spells produce a great deal of tension among villagers. Except for guarding their fields and obtaining water, there is little for the male villagers to do during this period. The women and children are tending the *chena* crops. Meanwhile, adult males will constantly be worried about their paddy fields and means to earn some quick income to pay off debts or other expenses. These are anxious months for villagers for they have invested so much of their energy and economic resources into their paddy fields. In this remote and dry area of Sri Lanka, drought, floods and/or wild boar or elephants can quickly destroy all one's efforts.

The Paddy Harvest

When the paddy shoots begin to bend from the weight of the seed and the fields turn a golden color, then is the time for harvesting. The harvest period extends from April through May. Sudden April rains are not uncommon. It becomes imperative for villagers to reap their fields during dry periods for the rain will mold and ruin their paddy seed. Harvesting is a time of tension and the work is done fast and through the night.

The work of reaping and threshing is done with a combination of *atam* and cash labor. Women collect the cut paddy stalks in bundles which are cut by the men and carried to the threshing floor. It is a common practice for wealthier villagers to contract this work out. Fields are measured in *moulans*; one *moulan* comprising an area of sixteen by seven arm lengths which is measured by a notched string.

Prior to reaping the paddy, a space for collecting the paddy stalks is cleared either in the field or in the house compound. This is considered a sacred area and the *lebbe* is enlisted to sanctify it. Prayers are recited and charmed water is sprinkled over the floor. Those in possession of an elephant's tooth will set it on floor. The elephant's tooth is said to function as a form of contagious magic, the quality of largeness possessed by the tooth is said to be magically transmitted to the paddy seeds. The charmed water and other magical rites also serve the purpose of protecting the area from the "greedy" eye of passers-by.

The paddy is collected in large mounds and covered with hay or a tarpaulin to protect against the rain and heavy wind. The paddy ricks are then left to dry for a few days prior to threshing.

To avoid "greedy" eyes and also because of the mild, cool climate, the arduous and long task of threshing usually begins in the early evening. The paddy stalks are pitched from the ricks to the floor with long forked wooden sticks and are then trampled by water buffalo or oxen, buffalo preferred because they are heavier. There is only room for two buffalo or oxen and teams are rented for twenty rupees per night.

The following day, straw is separated and women are hired or obtained on *atam* to winnow the paddy seed from the stalks and chaff. This is an arduous and time consuming process. A few villagers used tractors for part of the winnowing process using the radiator fan as a blower. The winnowing women were paid either in paddy or in cash. Payments in paddy were usually preferred for they were more remunerative. Women had the option of accepting seven rupees per day or one *marikar* of unhusked paddy. One *marikar* is equivalent to three measures of rice and one measure of rice cost between three and six rupees, thus women could earn the equivalent of nine to eighteen rupees by selecting payment in paddy.

After the harvest, paddy is stored in gunny sacks in the home. Paddy will either be sold at the Paddy Marketing Center (five miles away) or to private entrepreneurs. Regardless of the amount of paddy harvested, a certain amount must be sold to repay debts and acquire needed cash for the upcoming festival season. Bushels of paddy are sold for a standard price at the Marketing Center.

In 1980, a bushel sold for forty rupees and in 1981 for seventy rupees. Villagers will sell inferior quality paddy, padded with straw, stones, dirt or wet, at the Marketing Center. Similarly, the managers of these Centers are typically accused of cheating when they weigh the bushels, skimming a measure or so for their own purposes. Private brokers and shop owners also bought paddy. Though the price is the same, the advantage of selling it to merchants is that villagers are sure the paddy will be weighed accurately. Paddy may also be sold on the black market, usually to merchants from the east coast who employed a villager in this capacity. In 1981, black market paddy was sold at seventy-five to eighty rupees per bushel and was said to be exported to India.

One informant explained the economic motive for selling paddy on the black market as follows:

> After the harvest there is plenty of paddy available all over Sri Lanka. Two or three months later the price of paddy will increase since there is less paddy available. It is then that villagers can sell their paddy for the most profit. However, people usually cannot wait that long for they must repay their debts.

Payments in paddy bushels must also be made to the two assistant agricultural officers in the village and to the mosque. The assistants receive one half bushel per acre; the *lebbe* and *moidenaar* must also be given one half bushel each per household. If these payments are not met, religious services may be withdrawn.

Paddy may also be disbursed among needy relations. Hadji, for example, gave ten bushels to each of his two married sisters, for their husbands had deserted them. Ishmael, Hadji's brother-in-law, also gave ten bushels to his parents. The giving of paddy to poorer relations is considered a form of *zakat*. *Zakat*, one of the five obligatory Islamic principles, is the giving of 2.5% of one's wealth to the poor. In Kotabowa there was no formalized distribution or calculation of *zakat*, villagers simply referred to distributions of paddy to their relations as "zakat" payments. Most villagers with enough paddy in stock will distribute some to their poorer relations (usually husbandless sisters or parents). These payments signify kinship bonds and obligations rationalized in terms of Islamic precepts.

Religious Vows Offered After the Harvest

Each household fulfills vows immediately after the harvest. Vows are made prior to the sowing of paddy seed and fulfilled after the harvest. All villagers proffer two vows (some more): one to the Saint Mohideen Abdul Cader and the other to Hyatt Nabi. Nabi literally means "prophet" and some villagers equate Hyatt Nabi with Jesus Christ, but he is usually conceived of as a saint. The performance of vows parallels the ritual practices of the Sinhalese Buddhists. A coin is bound in a piece of cloth, a vow (*muradhi*) is offered and the coin is then tied to a tree or stored in the house. Vows are made for rain, the protection of the crops and for a large harvest.

The ritual resolution of both these vows differs. For Hyatt Nabi, each family brings banana leaves filled with sweet rice to the mosque where it is distributed among those present. The *lebbe* and others will recite a short prayer prior to the distribution. Villagers will bring the *pukkha* (rice offering) during the evening of any day.

The vow for Mohideen involves a large feast. Mohideen is the most well-known and powerful of the saints. For this vow, the mosque officials, important kinsmen (father, father-in-law, brothers), a few friends and village leaders are invited to the household for an evening meal. One informant noted that it was important to invite a balanced number of consanguineal and affinal male kin. Prior to the meal, the *lebbe*, *moidenaar*, *maulevi* and other religious figures will sit under a canopy of saris on a white cloth inside the house and recite a set of prayers in Tamil as well as Arabic. The prayers in Tamil specifically address and praise Abdul Cader.

After prayers, the head of the household will hand a few coins in turn to each of those who participated in the prayers. This is a nominal payment and no one will look to see how much was given (usually a rupee or less). An extravagant dinner is then served with meat and vegetable curries. After the meal, the host offers cigarettes (or if poor, *bidis*) to all the guests. The guests will usually only stay until they have finished smoking their cigarette. Men appear to be uncomfortable chatting idly inside a private home for they are used to congregating at public social arenas, their fields or the mosque.

The religious significance of vows for cultivation was explained by Adam Marikar in the following tale:

> There were two brothers who were very successful farmers, collecting huge harvests annually. They decided that proffering vows was a foolish waste of time and expense. That year they proceeded to cultivate without offering any vows. Their crops died; the following year they again refused to offer vows and their fields withered once more. Thereafter they prayed for forgiveness and gave a large *kandhoori* [religious almsgiving cum feast]. That year they offered vows and their harvests were bountiful.

While vows may or may not help in producing satisfactory harvests, villagers believed that they are certain to be unsuccessful without them. Thus, vows serve as a kind of insurance policy: by remembering Allah, the Prophet and the saints through vows, the saints, in behalf of Allah and the Prophet, favor their devotees with rain and protection from the environment. Vows help to assuage the feelings of anxiety villagers feel over climatic and environmental variables over which they have no control. The saints are asked to protect fields and bring the rains. The fulfillment of the vows to Mohideen and Hyatt Nabi re-affirm those bonds of social identity as Muslims and as kinsmen that may have been strained or neglected during the cultivation season.

Conflicts During the Paddy Season

The cultivation officer estimated that fifty percent of the conflicts during the paddy season were over water, twenty-five percent over cattle damaging fields and twenty-five percent over other issues. Conflicts over water rights were endemic during the paddy season. Below disputes over water, *atam* arrangements, *adee* and mortgage transactions will be described.

1. Conflicts over water rights

Most disputes over water rights center around lands in the *deniya* area near the *maditawa* tank. As mentioned earlier, the *maditawa* tank was intended to irrigate eighty acres of new paddy lands; instead,villagers cleared and cultivated three hundred acres.

Annually, two assistants to the agricultural officer are elected. These assistants (*vel vidanes*) are expected handle minor disputes, distribute literature and new information on cultivation methods, inform villagers of the time schedules to prepare their fields and regulate the allocation of irrigation water from the *maditawa* tank.

The local *vel vidanes* have little actual authority to implement any of these tasks. For example, Adam Lebbe complained that the owners of the paddy lands nearer the tank were diverting the waters before it reached his field on the days he was assigned to receive water. He voiced his grievance with the agricultural officer who referred him to Mohideen, one of the *vel vidanes*. Meeting with Mohideen at a shop, Adam Lebbe explained that he had not received water on the day allotted him. Mohideen replied, "I can't help it. You will have to wait your turn. I cannot open another channel especially for you...whoever has the strength takes the water; whatever orders I give no one listens, so what am I to do?" At that time, the Waede Mahatteya said facetiously, "I am going to take water right now," and turned to go. Mohideen replied, "yes, that is the way." In this way, the legitimate authorities explicitly approved the unregulated (and illegal) commandeering of water.

2. Dispute Over Atam Arrangements

Siddik and Farook, both in their twenties, were close friends who cooperated in business and labor activities. Every year they shared *atam* work with one another during the paddy cultivation. In 1981, Farook had worked on Siddik's paddy field for four days, bringing a team of oxen for plowing. At the time Siddik was scheduled to begin helping Farook, Siddik's elder brother requested him to come to Bakinigehavela where he lived. Siddik's brother was a bus driver and had taken a leave of absence to plow his paddy fields and urgently needed Siddik's help. Siddik explained his position to Farook who sympathized and they agreed to delay work on Farook's field for four days. Farook also loaned Siddik two oxen to help with the plowing on his brother's field. Four days went by and Farook went to Bakinigehavela to find Siddik and ask for his oxen back so that he could continue his own plowing. Siddik said that he needed the oxen for an additional day and offered to pay for both the use of the oxen and the *atam* work Farook had done. Farook was furious because he needed to have his fields plowed more than he needed the money. Siddik gave him the oxen back and the following day went to fulfill his *atam* obligations with Farook.

Farook and Siddik remained angry with one another; Farook because he felt that Siddik had taken advantage of their friendship, and Siddik because Farook had not considered his obligations to his brother or accepted the financial offer for compensation. During the following months both avoided any social contact with one another. Both were friends of mine and when one came to visit the other would immediately leave. Neither confronted each other nor brought the matter to public notice. Eventually the two began to talk and the dispute simply ended over time.

While this dispute is a trivial example of disputes over *atam* arrangements, it does highlight the potential strain inherent in the system. Atam networks are developed in two ways: (1) over time, stable networks become established between relations, friends and cultivators in adjacent fields; (2) additional *atam* laborers are often sought immediately by visiting at the shops or other public arenas and soliciting those interested in establishing a temporary *atam* alliance. Individuals who acquire a reputation for not fulfilling *atam* exchanges of labor are unlikely to find villagers willing to establish permanent or temporary *atam* exchanges. External contingencies, as in Siddik's case, can produce overlapping and contradictory demands on individuals.

Siddik, caught between the demands of his brother and his obligation to Farook, opted to compromise in favor of his brother. Farook checked his anger by avoiding rather than confronting Siddik because of their friendship and the importance of reliable and long term *atam* relationships.

Atam networks are part of the cultural tradition for recruiting labor where few villagers have the necessary capital to hire laborers. The continuity of *atam* networks is based on mutual trust between members. The reliance of villagers on these networks and the implied threat that they would not be able to recruit *atam* labor in the future serves to mitigate this potential strain.

3. Dispute Over ***Adee***

In 1958 Koostapel, the retired village headman, had given nine bushels of paddy land to Omar (Adam Marikar's son). At the time, Koostapel was in his fifties, his only daughter was already married and he already owned forty bushels of paddy fields. Koostapel had intended to give this land to his youngest son, Hassan, after he married (Hassan was about ten years old in 1958). The land given on *adee* had been dowry land divided between Koostapel's wife and her sister. The sister's husband was deceased and was supported by Koostapel. Initially, Omar gave the *adee* payment to Koostapel and his sister-in-law. Subsequently,Koostapel's sister-in-law sold her half-share of paddy land to Omar for two thousand rupees. In the 1960's, Omar began to give the *adee* payments to Hassan. Hassan married in 1970 and, since his father was old and infirm, took over his father's paddy lands. Omar continued to work his land and give annual *adee* payments to Hassan without incident.

In 1977 Omar neglected to give his *adee* payment. Apparently, Hassan contacted the police and they ordered Omar to pay the *adee*, which he did. Omar then offered to buy the land from Hassan for four thousand rupees. Hassan countered, asking for seven thousand rupees and Omar, according to Hassan, agreed. Hassan began to make arrangements to build a new house and re-tile the roof of his old house. Omar, in the meantime, had changed his mind. He argued that he had single-handedly constructed a small dam by the paddy field at a cost of five thousand rupees and wanted the sum subtracted from the price. Omar continued to work the land through 1979 giving *adee* payments to Hassan. Omar refused to return the land to Hassan or buy it for seven thousand rupees.

In 1979 Hassan contacted the cultivation officer and Omar was ordered to return the land to Hassan on the condition that Hassan reimburse Omar for the dam with an, as yet, unspecified sum. Hassan went to the irrigation department in Moneragela in order to obtain a certificate stating that the dam was built by them. This was a subtle point, since the dam built by Omar was an extension of the culvert overpass constructed by the irrigation department. In 1980 a court case was filed by Hassan against Omar. Before the case came to trial Omar gave the land back to Hassan.

Villagers were reluctant to file and proceed with court cases. Hassan, as the village headman's son, was better educated than most villagers and was familiar with government agencies and their functions. Omar, though a leader in the village, was not adept at maneuvering in nor knowledgeable of government agencies. Within the village boundaries, Omar was the dominant of the two, Hassan was a meek person who avoided social interactions in the village. As long as the dispute remained within the village arena, with local-level authorities such as the agricultural officer, Omar could successfully contend with Hassan. Hassan's strategy changed the rules for resolving the dispute, transferring the forum of arbitration from a local to a national level.

An inherent strain in long-term *adee* contracts is, of course, that the lessee begins to think of the land as "his." Omar had worked this land for twenty years. The paddy land was near the stream dividing Kotabowa and Godigamuwa and by building a dam he had substantially increased the productivity of the land. On the other hand, Hassan owned the land and had legitimate rights to re-claim the land at any time. Within the village such disputes may be resolved by clout (e.g., Omar refusing to acknowledge Hassan's claim) or arbitrated by local level agents familiar with the history of the dispute and with the moral as well as legal contentions of the disputants.

4. Dispute Over Mortgaged Paddy Land

In 1978, Meera Saibo had mortgaged one acre of paddy land to Pitchai for one thousand rupees. Meera Saibo was employed as a mechanic at the C.T.B. (Ceylon Transportation Board). He had married Pitchai's sister and had obtained his job through Pitchai's alliance with the regional MP (Member of Parliament). All public sector jobs are funneled through the MP and consequently distributed among the MP's supporters. For this reason, Pitchai received the paddy land for a low mortgage.

In 1979, Pitchai collected a ninety bushel harvest from this paddy field. Meera Saibo had asked Pitchai if he could work the land the following year even though it was still mortgaged. Pitchai agreed with the stipulation that Meera Saibo give him ten bushels after the harvest, double the normal *adee* payment.

Pitchai cultivated a paddy land adjacent to the mortgaged land. In 1980, Meera Saibo had collected his harvest in paddy ricks. Pitchai's son, about twelve years old, had apparently gone out in the evening to watch his father's field. He had been carrying a torch and embers from the torch, caught by the wind, had set fire to Meera Saibo's harvest.

Meera Saibo contacted the agricultural officer and they met with Pitchai. Pitchai agreed to pay five hundred rupees in compensation. Only a part of Meera Saibo's harvest had been burned and the agricultural officer, and villagers, agreed that five hundred rupees was a generous offer by Pitchai.

In 1981, the following year, Pitchai refused to allow Meera Saibo cultivate the land until he repaid the entire mortgage. Meera Saibo lodged a complaint at the police station in Bibile accusing Pitchai of threatening him with a rifle. No action was taken by the police. On a subsequent evening, at the village central shopping node, Meera Saibo publicly accused Pitchai, in Sinhalese, of being a "kapande yaluwa" ("cutting friend", hence someone who would "cut" his own friend to gain an advantage). He then accused Pitchai's son of deliberately setting fire to the paddy rick. He argued that Pitchai had asked his son to set fire to the paddy rick so that he, Meera Saibo, would not be able to pay off the mortgage. In this way Pitchai would be able to keep the land permanently when the time clause in the mortgage contract expired.

During this diatribe, Pitchai remained standing impassively. As Meera Saibo approached him, Pitchai backed up and stood on a log in front of his own shop. From this position, surrounded by allies, Pitchai began his own verbal assault saying, "If you step into that field you will find your mistake. I'll take your flesh off your bones and return it to you...without paying me *adee* for the last two years, how can I allow you to work the land? I have paid a solid one thousand rupees in cash. This year I am not going to give the land to anyone. On the day you pay me back, you can have the field." At this time some of Meera Saibo's relations appeared and led him back to his house.

Pitchai was a politically ambitious man; he was a political broker, an assistant agricultural officer and president of one of the two Rural Development Committees. To develop and maintain this network of allies, Pitchai adopted a variety of tactics: he obtained employment for villagers, gave loans, spoke in behalf of the village and individuals to the MP and other government agents, and held a large almsgiving at his house annually where he fed the villagers and outside guests. The mortgage agreement had further highlighted Meera Saibo's indebtedness to Pitchai. Pitchai had also profited from the mortgaged land, the 1979 harvest of ninety bushels being equivalent to thirty-six hundred rupees.

Meera Saibo's wrath centered around economic concerns—the burning of part of his harvest and the fear that Pitchai's underlying motive was to acquire the mortgaged land. The Waede Mahatteya, commenting on the dispute, said, "All the Sinhalese and villagers of this town are disgusted with Pitchai because he wants everything for himself. With his large mouth he wants to rule the entire village, all because he is on good terms with the MP." Meera Saibo and the Waede Mahatteya's comments crystallize the "Achilles heel" of political brokers: their affiliation with national level politicians produces a growing distrust in the community of the motives of these brokers. To become a successful political broker depends on being able to provide a large voting bloc for the MP. This voting bloc is developed through the tactics described above. The successful political broker's wealth will increase dramatically since he has control over local level resources provided by the government (i.e., jobs, development contracts, agricultural subsidies, ability to obtain land deeds and business permits, etc.). The political broker is then in danger of being perceived by villagers as a local level robber baron. If this perception becomes crystallized through a series of disputes between the broker and villagers, he may lose his constituency and his role as a broker.

Pitchai's concerns in this dispute were much wider than Meera Saibo's. Pitchai was motivated not only to keep Meera Saibo and his family in his network of supporters, but also to stop any public grumbling about his "greed." Pitchai's generous offer of five hundred rupees and his eventual offer to give the land to Meera Saibo's brother were, in the context of the dispute, more than generous. This public display of magnanimity in contrast with Meera Saibo's emotional outburst was also an effective strategy for suppressing the expression of similar sentiments by the villagers. As a political broker, Pitchai could ill afford for Meera Saibo's accusations to attain some level of legitimacy, nor did he wish to lose Meera Saibo as an ally cum client. Further, because of the economic importance of land as an economic resource, Pitchai had to shift the emphasis of the quarrel from the more emotionally salient and economically threatening issue of Meera Saibo losing the mortgaged land to the narrower issue of *adee* payments. Pitchai's argument centered around Meera Saibo neglecting to pay *adee*, while Meera Saibo's argument suggested that Pitchai had deliberately, through his son, set fire to the harvest in order to eventually acquire the land through legitimate means (i.e., the mortgage agreement). In light of all that, Pitchai had much to gain—community praise for his generous and compassionate behavior, re-establishing a patron-client relationship with Meera Saibo (and his brother) and perhaps, in the future, ownership of a fertile paddy land. Speculation over whether or not the fire was set deliberately had to be squelched. Pitchai accomplished this by conducting himself first as a leader with physical clout ("I'll take your flesh off"), secondly by establishing the legitimacy of his position and finally by demonstrating his compassion. Pitchai kept the conflict from escalating by keeping it personal. By giving the land to Meera Saibo's brother on *adee*, he further limited the potential for any escalation of the conflict.

Conclusion

A villager tersely expressed the socio-economic centrality of cultivation as follows: "without a *mammoty* (hoe) there is no cultivation, without cultivation there is no money, without money there is no God." Doubtless he did not mean to imply that the existence of God depends on the a priori existence of the *mammoty*. His intention was to emphasize that the community could not exist without cultivation and, dead, they cannot worship God.

The environmental prerequisites for the maintenance and continuity of the village were land and water. As Leach wrote,

> But the Pul Eliya community does not only operate within an established framework of legal rules, it also exists within a particular man-made ecological environment. It is the inflexibility of topography—of water and land and climate—which most of all determines what people shall do (1961:9).

The organizational principles of social life during the paddy season are adaptive responses to these environmental realities. The *adee*, and to a lesser extent, mortgaged land systems were effective mechanisms for distributing land in a peasant economy where cash resources were scarce. Similarly, the *atam*, reciprocal labor exchange, networks functioned as an effective institution for recruiting stable and temporary laborers in a "low-cash" economy. Both the *atam* and *adee* systems have been adapted to the increasing incursions of a cash-based economy. Laborers had the option of being paid in kind (with *atam* labor), cash or in paddy. Adee transactions could also be made either in cash or bushels of paddy.

Ideal models and normative patterns of behavior were presented as "guidelines," not as fixed prescriptions for behavior. Villagers adapted these models to fit their own resources. Individual variations of these behavioral patterns (or models) were limited by social and environmental constraints. Atam labor should be reciprocated, otherwise one cannot recruit *atam* laborers in the future. The development of the *maditawa* tank opened up new lands for paddy cultivation. However, at the same time the uncontrolled clearing of three hundred acres led to the breakdown of regulatory mechanisms to distribute the water. The present anarchic condition whereby villagers simply break the tank gate open and let the water run has produced a context of pervasive and endemic conflict.

THE FESTIVAL SEASON

Introduction

The festival season is defined as that period of time (or season) between the end of the paddy harvest and the beginning of the *chena* season. The festival season could be labelled the wedding season, the business season, the leisure season, or the desperate season. Indeed, the season may be truly desperate for those without paddy fields or those whose harvests have been poor. With the end of the rains, the water table falls until by July only one or two wells may fill with a few inches of water during the night. Each year during the festival season women were forced to dig into the dried-up riverbed for water. Bathing, washing clothes, and transporting water became arduous chores due to the lack of water.

During the two aforementioned cultivation seasons, villagers have neither the time nor funds to be pre-occupied with non-cultivation chores. Though religious ceremonies occur during the other seasons, they are determined by the Islamic calendar and are poorly attended. For most villagers, this period between cultivation periods is a time of revitalization, of increased religiosity, of festivals, and of weddings and maturation rites. Villagers do not ignore economic activities during the festival season, but they must turn to a variety of temporary economic ventures not associated with cultivation *per se*.

The festival season, roughly the period from April to August, is the richest and most varied period of this annual cycle. It is a period of "leisure": of rest, games, music, and recreation; of injecting a sense of mutual joy, pleasure and camaraderie into personal relationships rather than the socio-economic network bonds that were emphasized during the cultivation seasons. It is also a period when new alliances and friendships are developed, often through marriage. It is also a time when villagers concern themselves with Islam. There is more time to go to the mosque for daily prayers and to sit around discussing religious matters or listen to others.

The festival season is divided into a series of distinct social activities that are discussed in their approximate temporal sequence. Immediately after the paddy is harvested, winnowed, stored and/or sold, many villagers participate in a series of *bajas* (colloquialism for parties). Circumcision rites and marriages only occur during the festival season. The local *Burdha* festival, the only village festival, occurs during this season. Finally, *Ramadan*, the month of fasting, marks the end of the festival period.

In May 1981 Hamsa discussed the festival season and the activities that people participate in over this period. His comments, while incomplete, present a picture of some of these activities and concerns:

> ...many (villagers) are now going to buy cows and bulls from the Sinhalese areas to sell here. During the festival season there are plans for marriage, *sunnuth* [circumcision for male adolescents], *danas* [almsgiving with food], business ventures, boutique openings, new houses started...life goes on.

This chapter does not lend itself to the natural organization that characterized the cultivation seasons and is organized as follows:the first section of this chapter is concerned with "leisure" activities such as games, parties, daily conversations and social interactions, and a pot-pourri of other recreational activities; the second section is concerned with circumcision and marriage rites, both of take place exclusively during this season; the third section concerns the *Burdha Kandhoori*, which did not take place in 1980 but resumed again in 1981; the fourth and final section concerns *Ramadan*, the month of fasting.

Villagers spend much of their time telling stories, mostly with a religious theme. The following tale, told by Farook and re-told by other villagers, seems to capture the flavor of the annual cycle in Kotabowa.

> One day a man was making a trip through the jungle. As he was walking he was stalked by a lion. The man started running and he came upon an old, unused well. He wanted to jump into it, but as he looked over the side he saw a huge cobra coiled and ready to strike on the floor of the well. Just as the lion approached, the man saw a vine hanging from a tree going into the well. Immediately, he caught hold of the

> vine and remained there caught between life and death, inside the well with the cobra below him and the lion above. While hanging there he looked up and saw a rat was busy gnawing at the vine he was hanging onto. He thought to himself, 'Oh God what has happened to me? What am I going to do?' There was nothing to do but die. While he was thinking a drop of honey fell into his mouth. The honey was so tasty, so sweet, he opened his mouth wider and wider trying to capture another drop of honey. Sipping the honey, he forgot everything else. This drop of honey is like a human being's life.

Farook went on to explain that the well is the grave, the lion is the devil who had come to take away life, and the honey is sexual happiness. This is an oft-repeated fable among villagers, and it is during the festival season that the drop of honey may be said to fall.

Leisure Activities

Shortly after the field has been harvested, impromptu "bajas" are held. The participants are males of any age who gather at the house of the sponsor who is expected to provide *bidis* (local cigarettes), sometimes tea and sweets. Hamsa, a twenty-nine year old cultivator and shop owner, held a *baja* in 1980. Present that evening were his brothers, two of his wife's brothers, and a core group of about fifteen males. The *baja* was held in an empty, newly erected room, in which the group sat in a circle along the wall. The party assembled at about 8:30 p.m. There had been no invitations since friends, relatives and those coming to Hamsa's boutique had been told about the *baja*.

Hamsa, fond of drums, played a long bongo drum; his elder brother, Bas, brought an autoharp, and the remainder of the villagers played on bottles with coins, clapped, beat against tables or chairs and sang. Usually the better singers were urged to sing while the others clapped, whistled, and formed the orchestra. No one appeared inhibited and, while one or two were shy, most attempted to sing a song. Other villagers, drawn to the noise, were invited by Hamsa to come in and share a cup of tea and a *bidi*. They either stayed and participated or lingered and left. The older men tended to stay a little while before departing. The *baja* continued until morning prayers at about 4:30 a.m. The three *bajas* that I attended all lasted till morning prayers and at none was alcoholic beverages present. The core members of the *baja* group tended to remain, though some fell asleep. Perhaps, since these are somewhat rare events, villagers wish to signify their freedom from the constraints of cultivation work by staying up till dawn enjoying themselves. It may also serve symbolically as a communal expression of leaving behind the constraints of work, and the renewal not only of camaraderie but of a common Islamic identity, as they go in unison to the Mosque for morning prayers, most for the first time in the year.

Other informal groups formed during the festival season. These groups were partially formed through kinship ties, but the majority seemed linked by friendship ties and common interests. These groups were recognizable as they would participate in various games together bathe with one another or simply mill around with one another.

I was intimately associated with one such group during my residency in Kotabowa. The group's members were all age mates between twenty-five and thirty-five years old and strong supporters of the Sri Lankan Freedom Party (the liberal party out of favor at the time). They were also all relatively enterprising and moderately well off by village standards. This recognizable group consisted of approximately ten core members, with twenty or so peripheral members. The most discernible link was their political affiliation. This group would often visit local Sinhalese villages to play volleyball. Typically they met at Hamsa's shop every night to gossip, joke, and discuss politics. During the cultivation season members of this group were not observably linked in economic cooperative ventures. However, members of this group who were also closely related as kin would extend this social affiliation to economic arenas.

There were other friend/kin/social groups. For example, youths involved in religious affairs tended to form another such friendship group. Males over forty seldom appeared to form large friendship groups, perhaps because they were too burdened with supporting large families. However, elder villagers did form friendship groups. The most obvious consisted of those elder males who had been or were functionaries of the mosque. The mosque served as an ersatz men's house where between the fourth call to prayer (*Maghrib*) at sundown and the fifth call to prayer (*Isha*) at about 8:15, these elder men would sit in the antechamber on mats and discuss religious questions, upcoming marriages, village affairs or simply told stories.

Various kinds of card games also occupied the time of many of the male villagers. These men could be found sitting in small circles at the end of a road or on the verandahs of houses playing very simple gambling games such as "odds or evens." More complex card games (similar to gin rummy) were also played.

Marbles were also a popular pastime, and on occasion bets were placed. Gambling was not excessive, though large sums of money had infrequently been lost or gained. It was said that one man in the village had become drunk, stolen his son's money and lost five thousand rupees to Ganja Haniffa, who was then forced by the villagers to return what he had not already spent. However, such large losses are an oddity, not the norm.

Villagers often took trips during this time to visit relatives in various parts of the island. Relatives of Kotabowans can be found in almost every section of the island, and these folks provide lodging and food, for it is an important aspect of social etiquette to entertain guests grandly. Most often only male villagers went on such journeys. Farook was an exception when he took his wife and four-year-old son on a trip to the east coast.

It was difficult for a male researcher to obtain extensive information on what women did for enjoyment. Their lives were relatively restricted and most of their time was spent taking care of daily chores. There did, however, appear to be women's social groups. One such female group was called a *seetu*. A *seetu* is an informal group in which each woman donates a particular item (e.g., sugar) or sum of money (e.g., five rupees) each week with one woman the recipient of the entire donation. Women also gather at each other's homes or at the well when they bathe and chat. Those who chew betel nut may spit nonchalantly to the side. Social interaction between men and women is frequent and casual and their public conversations are usually laced with sexual innuendoes. Shy women will avoid public interactions with men. However, the less shy women appear very comfortable in the company of men. For example, the following was an exchange that took place in front of my house: a man, Abdul Aseez, was walking down the road when he saw the *Lebbe*'s 20-year-old daughter weeding the front lawn of her house. As he went by he said "Nelle saman," meaning—"good stuff." In reply she said "Of course, the 'stuff' is *sanghu* mark." *Sanghu* is the trade label for a company that makes quality saris. The publicly made remark was not intended as a sexual advance but merely as a joke, and was understood as such by those nearby.

It is during festivals that women have the best opportunity to enjoy themselves. I visited the towns of Jailany and Kalmunai during the festival period for the two saints, Mohideen Abdul Cader and Meera Saibo (also known as Shaul Hamid). Muslim families from all over Sri Lanka would make pilgrimages to the shrines of these Saints. Pilgrimages are overtly religious activities, but they are also viewed as culturally acceptable means for women to go on holidays. Pilgrimage sites offer ample opportunities for men and women to flirt with one another. This was obvious as the pilgrimage sites are also market sites where all sorts of jewelry, household utensils, clothes and foods are sold. During the evenings, men and women dressed in their finest make the rounds as the loudspeakers constantly exhort the crowd to keep their collective mind on the religious nature of the event. Of the people interviewed at both festivals, not more than twenty percent had any idea of who the Saint was who was being honored. A typical response was that of a man who said, "I came with my family just to see the place and have a good time. It is a good opportunity for us to talk and be friendly so if we go to other places we will know some people...we came in a tour bus."

At Kalmunai, the retired Member of Parliament, explained to me in English,

> Almost everyone from the Kalmunai area comes here [to the festival]. This is not like America where there are so many things to do and a festival like this would not attract a crowd. Here, there is nothing to do so the people come. The festival may increase in popularity but that does not mean that there is a corresponding increase in religious fervor. Even people who think such things as religious vows are useless come and

drop a coin or two in the till box because, simply, it's the only place in town.

Most villagers in Kotabowa cannot afford to visit the Kalmunai festival, although it coincides with the end of the harvest season (in late April). In 1981 only four Kotabowans (all males) visited Kalmunai during the festival season. Similarly, only four visited Jailany in February for the festival for Abdul Cader. However, annually approximately fifty villagers, men and women, attend the Kataragama festival, which takes place during the festival period. This is a predominantly Hindu-Buddhist festival, the largest in Sri Lanka and a mosque is located adjacent to the main festival grounds.

Aside from pilgrimages, games, *bajas* and other parties, most of the leisure time for males is spent around the tea boutiques and small general shops. Men of all ages congregate and sit and talk for hours while chewing betel or smoking *bidis*. There are two major shopping centers in the village: one at the junction and one in the central area (see the Kotabowa map). The central area is the busiest since it is between the junction and the mosque. It is also centrally located in relation to most of the dwellings. There are five shops at the central area with a sixth about one hundred yards further down toward the mosque. Of the five shops one is a tea boutique and the other four are general stores. Figure 5 below is a sketch of the central area, disregarding residential buildings.

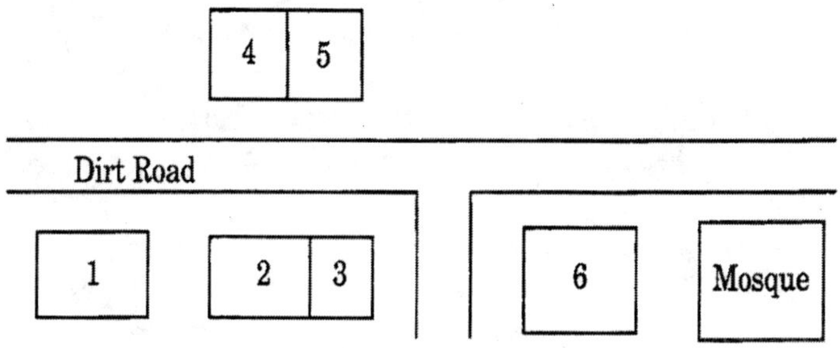

Figure 5. Central Area of Kotobowa

Of the six boutiques illustrated only Hamsa's (no. 4) and Razak's (no. 2) remained continually open during my stay in Kotabowa; they are by far the most successful boutiques in Kotabowa. Except for Haniffa's tea boutique (no. 3), the shops are owned by influential and important men in the village. Both Hamsa and Haniffa received their shops as part of the dowry. Razak is the son of the snake doctor, who originally built the store and ran it most of the time. Razak's wife worked daily behind the counter; she was the only woman in the village who worked in the public eye. Pitchai's store (no. 5) is cyclical, open some weeks and closed others. Neither Pitchai nor Mohideen (no. 6) seemed to be particularly concerned about profiting from their respective stores. Both were involved in numerous outside ventures and both used their stores as meeting places to transact other more profitable business deals and as a means to establish patronage over more indigent relations and villagers. Similarly, Ishmael used his shop as a place to buy *bidi* leaves collected locally and sell them to outside merchants. Ishmael was one of the major brokers for *bidi* leaves in the village, and had established enduring ties with outside merchants.

Only Hamsa and Razak earned an income from their shops and were the only ones who kept their shops open during my three year residency in Kotabowa. Hamsa was a very affable man with a reputation for honesty and was also the mosque treasurer. He attributed the success of his shop to the fact that he always tried to greet customers with a joke and a smile, frequently passing out candy or *bidis*. Razak did not have Hamsa's verbal charm but his father, the snake doctor, did. The snake doctor was a mainstay at the shop and oversaw the business, he would call people over and invite them for a betel chew or *bidis*. His status as a medical healer and his sociable nature seemed to ensure a steady clientele. Razak's wife was also charming and attractive shopkeeper and undoubtedly attracted her share of customers to the store.

Stores in Kotabowa, as elsewhere in Sri Lanka, are central social nodes. The shops are also important meeting places for business deals, soliciting loans and seeking employment. When villagers feel a need to talk to someone in the shop area privately, they will simply make a "psst" sound and signal with the hand, palm downward, for the person to come. This occurred frequently and appeared to cause little disturbance to those remaining behind. The two or three called would gather a distance away from the hubbub, discuss whatever, and then return to join those hanging about. Though this might appear an unusual breach of sociability, it was an accepted practice, perhaps because privacy is situationally created rather locationally predicated.

Shop conversations center on one's present problems and plans, local, national and international politics, religion and village affairs. However, less serious topics of conversation such as swapping stories or discussions about sex were frequent. While this swapping of stories and joking about appears trivial when compared to cultivation procedures, marriages, religious rites etc., they have an intrinsic social utility without which life would certainly be more Hobbesian in nature. Free from the social constraints imposed by the necessities of subsistence, villagers could afford to let their "guards down" and simply enjoy the moment with their fellow villagers.

One such conversation which appealed to me is loosely translated below. This conversation took place between the *Lebbe*, Adam Marikar (both of whom are religious leaders) and "Loose" (his actual nickname given to him for his unconventional nature). The *Lebbe* and Marikar had been trying to explain to Loose about Islam and the Tablik movement (Muslims, usually well-to-do, who travel in the backwaters of Sri Lanka preaching orthodox Islam to the indigenous Muslims).

In response to their erstwhile explanation Loose said, "Because of Allah I can't sit and listen to everyone who wants to mention his name. I am a faithful believer in Allah but what if I am walking by myself down the road and some drunken man tries to attack me? What am I to do then? Am I to explain to Allah? You know what I'll do? I'll kick him right in the face."

The *lebbe* said that such action would be completely wrong, "Allah advised that you should ignore such people and mind your own business. That's the only way you can be true to Allah; only that way can you acquire merits. You will have to try to avoid such situations and walk in the right path. The world is like a cinema; it is temporary. By giving to human beings all things that are good and bad Allah is watching the show and checking if human beings choose the right things. For this reason we will have to be terribly careful; we must only select good things."

To which Loose replied, "If it is a drama then there should be all sorts of unwanted things and fights only then will the show be truly fantastic. Only for this reason, to be entertained, Allah creates fights and drunkards, therefore there is no wrong in my fighting."

At this point everyone burst into laughter. The *lebbe* replied, "People who disobey Allah's orders are punished by Isra'el Alai Salaam." Then Loose said, "Who is that man? What will he do? Not only you or I, the man who does evil, but everyone will be dying. It is true,is it not, that no one knows what happens after death, so who cares?"

Again everyone laughed. Marikar then responded, "Don't you talk like that, or you will be a terrible sinner by saying such things. Not only that but here, listen! My father had been the strongest man here at one time. One day he was talking just like this and scolded Isra'el Alai Salaam. The following day he went mad and started running about begging forgiveness for his sins. Thereafter he was cured, so you can see how he was punished."

Loose said, "How do you know the punishment was for this reason? Your father could have done some other nonsense." Again everyone laughed and he continued, "I don't care even if you are the *Lebbe* or Marikar, if the devil comes inside me I might even attack you so just go away...If everyone believes your admonitions no one would be able to stay alive. If someone is coming down the road to hit me and I hide from him then he will definitely come with others to my house and create a nuisance so it is best to face him on the road itself. That is what I am doing now...anyway tomorrow I will try to heed your advice, I will take a pound of *ganja* on the bus saying 'Allah, Allah' all the time to see what happens." With that final acerbic comment the conversation ended.

As social meeting places, the village marketplace and shopping nodes permit the freedom of expression with minimal risk of condemnation. Social tensions may be released, and novel or risky ideas may be expressed. The reason why Loose's heretical remarks were greeted with laughter rather than anger was due to the social context of the situation. In other contexts, similar remarks evoke quick rebukes. For example, on one occasion when a groom was being led to his bride's house, the accompanying crowd spontaneously changed from singing the traditional religious wedding songs to singing "baja" songs and were immediately reprimanded by the *lebbe*. In another situation, a man was sitting in the antechamber of the mosque between prayers. As people talked casually he inadvertently stretched his feet so that they were facing Mecca and he was immediately rebuked. On yet another occasion,between prayers a group of men had been admonished for discussing business rather than religious concerns. Loose's comments were perhaps not the result of deep philosophical introspection but highlighted to the extreme, and to the ridiculous in the eyes of the villagers, the pragmatic problem of being a good Muslim while at the same time dealing with the exigencies of making a living.

The example of Loose is reminiscent of Goffman's analogy of "behind the stage" behavior, where the make-up and the masks are removed and there is no script. The difference between the villagers "backstage" behavior as contrasted with their "onstage" behavior was most apparent to me during my first few months of residency in Kotabowa. During my initial wanderings through the village, topics of conversation frequently changed and arguments immediately subsided until it became too difficult for villagers to maintain this facade. The problem of sustaining a social "face" vis-a-vis outsiders presented itself on numerous occasions. Concern about limiting conflict situations to the realm of village affairs has been mentioned. It was also important for villagers to present a generalized image of community well-being to outside Muslims. For example, on a day that there was to be a funeral service for an old and impoverished man, a group of Muslims from Colombo had arrived in a van as representatives of the Tablik movement. They had come to preach about Islam and exhort villagers to attend the mosque for daily prayers and to participate in this movement. Their headquarters during their stay was the mosque. It is customary for Muslims to bury their dead on the day of death and the corpse is brought to the mosque on the way to the cemetery. At the mosque a *dos* (verses from the Koran in behalf of the dead) is recited by the *Lebbe* or other religious official. It is also customary for the family of the dead person to give money to those who recite these verses. The *Lebbe* suggested that *dos* should be recited at the home where the dead body was being cleansed and clothed because "the Jammat (Tablik) people are here and the family will have to pay for prayer recitements. So all of our poverty will come out in the open as they...(the family of the dead)...would only be able to give a little."

Ishmael argued that it was not good to recite *dos* "here by the house where it is dirty and near to the dustbin. *Dos* is part of the Koran and must be recited in the mosque; not just where you prefer."

The *Lebbe* and other religious leaders remained adamant and the *dos* was recited at the house. None of the Tablik people attended the funeral and were perhaps totally unaware of the procession and burial.

Regardless of the *Lebbe*'s motives or success in presenting a desired social impression for the Tablik members, his actions signified a bond of commonality between the individual and the community: the poverty of the dead man's family would also reflect the poverty of the entire village. The level of poverty in the village was self-evident but the *Lebbe* and others wished to avoid any social exhibition which would have to be shamefacedly acknowledged in their encounters with the Tablik groups. In this instance, the reputation of the village was thought to be reflected in the actions of the villagers. Whether or not the villagers agreed with the *Lebbe*'s decision, no one proposed the argument that the inability of the dead man's family to disburse a sufficient donation to the reciters solely reflected one family's poverty rather than on the entire village.

Loose could belittle Islamic concepts in the intimacy of the village arena since only his personal reputation was at stake, and his nickname is evidence of the lack of respect he is accorded by villagers. His remarks would have been less likely to be condoned in the presence of prestigious outsiders. The ability to read the social text in terms of condoning backstage behavior (through which religious dogma may be criticized or debated and fun can be poked at one another's poverty or ignorance) and shift to more formalized patterns of behavior in other contexts demarcated the insiders (i.e., the villagers) from the outsiders (i.e., the audience).

Even when social roles are relaxed, villagers remain aware of them. For example, should a respected person approach a crowd gathered at a shop, those sitting would stand and conversations would quickly shift from risque to more mundane matters. Also, in the presence of elder male relatives, those junior would also display a variety of deferential behaviors such as standing, not talking or smoking. Elder female relatives, including mothers, would not be shown similar deference except that sex would not be a topic of conversation. However, even these formal rules could be relaxed depending on the personalities of those of high status. Adam Marikar and the Snake Doctor, both respected elderly people, loved to joke and talk about sex and their presence did not evoke tokens of formal deference in terms of topics of conversation; they were, however, inevitably offered a seat by someone who had previously been sitting.

In concluding this section I have attempted to show some of the kinds of "unstructured" leisure activities that Kotabowans engage in, and, to a limited extent, to discuss their social value. I have emphasized the playful and sociable nature of these varied activities, and presented them as intrinsic to the web and woof of village life. These leisure activities enhance what may otherwise be viewed as a rather drab existence. I have also hoped to convey, however briefly,was the shared knowledge of villagers as members of a community who consensually perceive nuances of their own behaviors as they vary contextually. This common understanding and recognition of the appropriateness or inappropriateness of behaviors depending on context marks each villager as a Kotabowan.

CIRCUMCISION RITES

Circumcision rites are a subset of the Islamic category of "sunnuth," an Arabic term denoting not only circumcision but the set of instructions, declarations and "rites of passage" which constitute Islamic customs. Sunnuth customs are said to be the Prophet's own religious declarations independent of and in addition to the Koran. The Koran is said to have been directly transmitted to the Prophet by the archangel Gabriel, while the Prophet was in a "divine state." The *sunnuth*, on the other hand, was formulated while the Prophet was in a "normal" state of being. The Koran is a product of divine revelation; the *sunnuth* is a product of a man, albeit a Prophet.

Circumcision rites are more colloquially termed *kaliyaanam*, which literally means marriage or wedding. Villagers may ask if you have attended the *kaliyaanam*, which, depending on the context, can refer to any rite of passage which should be religiously ordained. *Kaliyaanam* connotes the festive sense of the rite as a celebration.

It is said that *sunnuth* transforms a boy into a man—a real Muslim, now permitted to enter the mosque. Uncircumcised boys may only enter the mosque vestibule and not the interior chamber where congregational prayer is performed. It was said that prior to circumcision, prayers are "not heard by God."

Usually, circumcision takes place for boys between the ages of ten and fourteen. There is some deviation, some boys being circumcised as early as six or as late as sixteen years of age. Prior to the circumcision, the boy should know all the essential Islamic prayers and procedures. In the days before circumcision, boys are quizzed by the *Lebbe*, *Marikar*, and *Maulevi* and asked to recite Yassim and Fatihah, two *suras* (chapters) in the Koran. After the boy has passed this exam, the religious officials are presented a gift by the parents, sometimes a cow but more frequently cash. The day for the circumcision is chosen by the *Lebbe*, who consults an almanac designating the most propitious days of the year.

The actual circumcision is performed by a man called the "Oosta Maama." There were no *Oosta Maamas* in the Kotabowa region and annually an *Oosta Maama* from the east coast is invited to perform the circumcisions of Muslim boys in Kotabowa. *Oosta Maama* denotes a person of low status and the name is often used to insult others. His unofficial "caste" status is expressed by the fact that the villagers avoid addressing him as *Oosta Maama* and that he eats separately from other villagers. *Oosta Maama* is a hereditary task, but not a full-time occupation. He is paid thirty-seven rupees per circumcision.

Of the four circumcision rites I witnessed, two were in May and the other two in July. At each of these rites more than one boy was circumcised. The morning of the rite the boy bathes, is fed a sweet rice porridge and is given a fine afternoon meal. Prior to the *sunnuth* he is dressed in new clothes. Wealthier parents will buy trousers and a new "western-type" shirt. Normally, however, a new sarong and white cotton shirt are worn. Prior to the ceremony the boy will be dressed by his friends and cousins while his elder brother(s) look on to give advice and encouragement. Scent is put behind the ears, the hair is oiled, a new *toppi* (or head covering) is placed on his head, and there is a feeling of excitement and camaraderie.

The house will have been decorated for the festivities. The room were the circumcision is to take place is cleaned, the floor pasted with a new coat of dirt, streamers hung from the rafters, and designs painted on the walls. The outside of the house is re-limed and decorated. Poles and ropes are set up with saris colorfully spread for a temporary canopy. Mats are cleaned and put underneath the canopy for the guests. Visitors come and go throughout the day, greeting the boy and giving him a few rupees either in an envelope or tucking them into his pocket. Before the evening prayers all the boys who are to be circumcised are led in procession to the two mosques where coin offerings are placed in the till boxes and the *Lebbe* leads the procession in prayers. *Baith* (religious songs) are sung as the procession makes its way through the streets. Finally, the boys are led to the house where the circumcision is to take place. These boys need not be close relatives and the house selected for the circumcision rites is usually belongs to the boy from the wealthiest family. The circumcision ceremony begins in earnest after the completion of evening prayers.

At 8:30 p.m., the mosque leaders will begin to arrive singing *Baith* to announce their coming to this joyous occasion. They are seated in a circle under the saried canopy. Seating arrangements for all such religious functions are more or less designated: the Marikars who are managers of the mosque rather than religious "virtuosos" sit on either side of the *Lebbe* and *Maulevis*. The Koran is placed in front of the *Lebbe* and Nauman Maulevi, who take the lead in the religious prayers and recitals. The rest of the guests take their seats around this inner circle. The women remain in the background, either in the house or engaged in cooking. Male relatives and friends take charge of the cooking of the rice and meat curries while the women the women are involved in the more mundane task of cleaning the rice, and preparing the vegetables and spices. The women remain uninvolved in the ceremonial aspects.

Fruits, and sweets are placed on the white linen around which the inner circle is formed. The fruits and sweets, called *narzi*, consist of papaya, pineapple, banana, rock candy, and sugar cane. Powdered incense is burned in a coconut shell and each guest, on arrival, takes a pinch of powder and places it in the shell. Male relations are in charge of serving the *narzi* and tea at regular intervals.

The boys remain outside in seclusion while the *mowlood* recitations (Islamic verses recounting the life and deeds of the Prophet Mohammed) begin. At about 11 p.m., they are led, one at a time, into the house where the circumcision takes place. The house has been purified and five or so males are inside with the *Oosta Maama*, including the father of each boy.

The first boy is invited in by the *Moulenaar* and he is told to lower his sarong and sit in a chair placed conspicuously center stage. As he sits, a man holds his arms and legs from behind. This man is never the father, but always an elder male relative. Meanwhile, the *mowlood* continues outside. Sitting solitary in a chair with an adult male's arms constraining the boy was too much for most; the boys would start to tremble and cry out. The *Oosta Maama* then pulls the foreskin out and places a clip, like a wood clothes pin, around it. The foreskin is quickly cut with a razor blade. Ash and other medicines are placed on the wound. The boys I saw were in tears, screaming "enne Wappa" (O, my father) over and over. They are lifted and placed on a mat and told to lie on their back. A white sheet is lowered by a string from the rafters forming a kind of cone so that the sheet would cover the boy without touching his wounded foreskin. The boys, sobbing and heaving, are continually consoled. Someone will use a piece of cardboard to fan the wound. After the *mowlood* recitals, friends and other concerned males will come and congratulate the boys.

The boys must remain inside the house until the wound heals, about seven days. During that time they are not to drink or eat very much, in order, according to villagers, to decrease the need to go to the bathroom. Visitors come daily to commend them on becoming "real Muslims" and may leave gifts.

I was told that the boys' female cross-cousins are the only females of the boy's generation permitted to visit and enquire about "their friend's health." Here "friend" had an overtly double meaning since the boys' are expected to eventually marry one of their cross-cousins who will afterwards become more intimately acquainted with their "friend."

On the day that the boys are permitted to leave the house they are given a large meal. Thereafter, the boys make the rounds through the village proudly holding their sarong out so it won't rub against their still sensitive foreskin. It was, to me, a somewhat befuddling and comic sight to see these adolescents strutting proudly through the village this way without a trace of embarrassment.

The essence of the circumcision ritual, the *sunnuth*, is a rite of passage into adulthood for boys and marks them as real Muslims. This is a direct adaptation of the Hebrew tradition which goes back to Ibrahim. The rite is also an ethnic marker in terms of purity and pollution, much more so in a country such as Sri Lanka where the male Buddhists and Hindus are not, as a rule, circumcised. The other purificatory markers associated with the *sunnuth* are (1) choosing a propitious day and time; (2) re-liming the house, preparing a new mud floor, and cleaning all the mats in the house; (3) the separation of women from the ceremony (because of religious/sexual significance and the possibility of menstruating women being present); (4) providing new clothes and a bath, (5) the presentation of sweets and fruits (*narzi*) during the *mowlood* service; and (6) the butchering of meats by the *Moidenaar*. The *sunnuth* ceremony reinforces the ethnic distinctness of the boys and Muslims present from the Sinhalese and Tamils in terms of religious behavior and ideology. The ceremony is termed a wedding, for it symbolically weds these boys not only with the Muslims of Kotabowa and Sri Lanka but with the Islamic world.

In terms of socio-political competition between villagers, religious ceremonies such as *sunnuth* offer the opportunity to express one's generosity toward the entire community (i.e., gift giving) in a religious context. The ceremony also offers the opportunity to display one's wealth and influence. During the actual ceremony such displays are subtle. The religious officials are given high priority. Important persons of the village and outsiders are served first and seated on mats while other villagers are seated peripherily on the ground or on older mats. At Pitchai's son's ceremony, the important merchants were seated in a separate room in the house and served goat and chicken curries by Pitchai and his brother. The remainder of the villagers, including the religious officials, ate from *sabhans* (large communal bowls).

After the dinner, the more prestigious people are offered cigarettes and the less prestigious, *bidis*. No one minds these differences, though sometimes comments are made. For example, when the cigarettes had run out, the Trustee (who always smokes cigarettes) joked about not having received any and pulled out his own. Pitchai quickly made amends by sending someone to the shop for an extra pack.

The *sunnuth* ceremony, as a rite of passage, expresses a diverse and complex combination of social values and relations: the legitimization of the boys' social identity as Muslims; the affirmation by the community of their Muslim identity as being distinct from other religious communities; the affirmation of unity and equality as founded on the two central themes of Islam-obedience to Allah and the equality of all Muslims; an opportunity to express one's social eminence in the village; and a projected expression signifying the pool of preferential marriage partners (i.e., the custom of female cross-cousins visiting the boys during their recovery and inquiring into the well-being of their "friend").

MARRIAGE

Marriage affects nearly every aspect of life in the village: as a social mechanism for regulating the distribution of resources from generation to generation, by expanding social networks, by the repetitive establishment of rules for interaction and behavior between people, by institutionalizing social roles and obligations and the division of labor. In short, the marriage ceremony is the social regulatory mechanism par excellence for the orderly transference of cultural ideology essential for the continuity of the society. These statements will be developed and expanded upon below.

Adolescence is a particularly difficult time for the women in the village. After they have matured, they are confined to the house and parents are reluctant to let their daughters go bathing or outside the domestic compound by themselves. Both men and women use the analogy of living in a "cage" or "prison" to describe this period in a woman's life.

In a questionnaire concerning the best and worst years of a person's life, women tended to answer as Kather Bibi, a 28 year-old woman, did: "During youth before puberty, when you are with your parents, is the best of times, and also after marriage when everything is still new." The worst times for both men and women are said to be after forty or so. Men and women both noted that "until you have children, there is no problem (in marriage), only when you have children do the difficulties begin." Male children are preferred because they will receive a dowry and can earn a living, female children are totally dependent on males for their economic and social security. Almost all of those questioned mentioned that the dowry is given to daughters because they are helpless; the dowry is to provide for them and their children. Another significant motivation in marriage arrangements was noted by an informant as follows: "The poor man will always try to raise his status by becoming better connected within the kinship network. Poor people do not wish to remain poor until they die, so they seek other people assistance through marriage ties."

The process of selecting a spouse involves a nexus of factors or criteria depending on the family's socio-economic and the age, appearance, and reputation of the woman or man in question. The ideal age for marriageable women is between seventeen and twenty, for men it is between twenty-five and thirty. However, men can marry at almost any age; after twenty-five or so it becomes nearly impossible to find a reputable husband for a woman.

Marriage arrangements should be initiated by the father of the bride, informally discussing the matter with boy's father. Formal meetings are held, once at the prospective groom's house and once at the bride's house in the presence of the *marikar*, *lebbe* and the elder men of the family. The dowry issue is bartered and resolved during these meetings with *marikars* acting as mediators. A date for the wedding is set, often as far as two years in the future.

There exists a proper age sequence in which children should marry. The daughters should marry first, starting with the eldest to the youngest, thereafter the eldest son to the youngest. If there is a wide discrepancy in age between the youngest daughter and the eldest son this sequence may be altered. For daughters this age sequence ought to be followed, for if a younger daughter marries prior to her elder sister, villagers will start to gossip and think something is wrong with the eldest daughter.

Though all marriages "should" be arranged, individual choice is recognized. The Mosque Trustee noted,

> Anyone who loves a woman will definitely marry that woman because he is going to live with her and not with her father. They can either elope or persuade the mosque officials to hold the marriage ceremony. Although it is preferable to have the father's consent, if the father doesn't agree than it can't be helped. The most important thing is that the Muslim religion strictly prohibits sexual intercourse prior to marriage.

Other villagers agreed with the Trustee's perceptions and Farook added:

> If this fact comes to light (that the man and woman love each other), the woman's family will be more interested (in a marriage) because their entire reputation is at stake. They will go to the man's family to discuss the matter. However, if the woman's family is poor they cannot go to the man's house for fear that they will demand too large a dowry. Therefore, they must somehow encourage the man (to marry the woman)...though parents arrange marriages, the couple must like one another...without affection no marriage takes place.

Marriage Selection

The two primary criteria for marriage selection are that the marriage partners be Muslims and that the couple are in a proper kinship relation with one another. These two criteria are not always sacrosanct, however. A woman in the 1970's was said to have married a Sinhalese man who had not converted to Islam. She had married him because her first husband, an outsider, had deserted her and returned to his natal village. She had also been under pressure from her father to marry who did not want to be economically burdened with her and her children. Divorced, deserted, or widowed women seldom have the opportunity to re-marry. After the man deserted the woman, she remained with her six children in the dowry house (from her first marriage) and supported her family with weaving mats and "koolie" work.

In another case of inter-religious marriage, a fairly prosperous villager who worked as a cattle broker for a Colombo meat merchant was married to a Muslim woman in Kotabowa. He was rumored, however, to have married a Hindu woman on the east coast where he worked. The Hindu woman came to the village once in search of her husband and a tremendous fight erupted between the two women. The man seldom resided in Kotabowa and his wife was also known to have "lovers." Even so, villagers appeared more bemused than angry about the situation. The Kotabowan wife did not file for divorce and apparently the situation remained as it was.

The Marikar provided the following description of the process for selecting a spouse:

> First, the parents of the woman try to find a man of the right age and character; someone who does not drink or smoke, and is honest and also somewhat educated. They try to figure out the kinship relation, whether or not the two can marry, and then inform me of their choice. Then I will go to the man's house and talk to the parents. I never say that the woman's parents asked about the availability of the man; I merely say that I think the man should marry that particular woman, whom I mention by name. We will discuss the amount of dowry to be expected. I go to the bride's parents and fix a date on a auspicious day for both parties to meet. The woman's parents go to the groom's house with a box containing bananas, various sweets and aluminum or copper vessels. Usually an elder member of the family or one of the parent's brothers goes as well. The *marikar* and the *lebbe* also accompany or a *maulevi* may go in place of the *lebbe*. The box is given to the groom's father, and a elder member of the groom's party opens it. The people receiving the box are not allowed to open it. The *marikar* acts as a witness to the amount of goods contained in the box. A Fatihah and other prayers are then recited by the *lebbe*. In the old days they would have a feast but this is no longer done. During this first visit the dowry is not discussed, only the availability of the man as a marriage partner. A date is then arranged for the man's father or elder male relation to go to the bride's house. At this session the *marikar* and the *lebbe* are also

present and the dowry discussion begins. The bride's father has numerous things to consider: first, he can only give what he has and second, he mustn't give more than he gave (or will give) to his other daughters; otherwise their husbands will become jealous. The third visit is arranged with the *marikar* and *lebbe* at which two more "big" people attend [the trustee and other *marikars*] and the dowry is usually finalized.

The Marikar's version is an idealized account. The Marikar criticized the dowry-bartering system because it is often with the greatest difficulty that the bride's family can amass the dowry. It was noted that if the groom's family should make the initial proposal both families should be of equal status, and the groom's family should not expect a large dowry, for it is they who have expressed the desire for the marriage.

Cross-cousin marriage arrangements are preferred because it keeps the "wealth in the family" and the two families have established long-term interdependencies with one another. As one informant explained, "I'll try to find a match (for my daughter) among my father's sister's children or mother's brother's children. This [the FaZi or MoBro children] is good because the affection won't fade between relations. The love will be there and the wealth will not go outside the family. If the daughter marries an outsider, he may sell the land and leave or fights may arise."

The snake doctor, Assaner Lebbe, explained the importance of cross-cousins marriages in terms of the helplessness of women. "Women are helpless. They can't climb trees, ask for money, do business, carry things, etc. Therefore they are given land (on dowry) and her father and brothers must look after her and protect her." There is greater risk involved if the daughter marries an outsider, who may dissipate the dowry wealth or lack affective ties with his wife's family. Marrying an outsider is also risky because of the higher possibility of desertion. Prolonged squabbles between the husband and his wife's family may lead to his departure from the village. Marriages between locals eliminates this possibility.

Below a number of case descriptions are provided to demonstrate the variety within the village of marriage patterns. These cases describe the range of strategies, motivations and disputes that occur in the process of selecting marriage mates.

Case 1. Kalender Lebbe explained the marriage of his son Siddik as follows:

> Siddik was involved with Aiath Mohideen's daughter. They [Aiath Mohideen's family] came to me in a decorated cart with fifty people and lots of presents. On that day we discussed the forthcoming marriage plans; a date was even fixed. The same month of these discussions, the girl attained puberty. This occurred after the marriage discussions, so I bought new clothes for her. When *Ramadan* came I also bought her clothes worth about five hundred rupees. All of a sudden a dispute arose between the parents and the marriage arrangements were canceled. They returned all of the clothes I had presented to them. Even so Siddik continued to visit this girl. With great difficulty I convinced him to stop seeing her. Some time later, my son became involved with Foxer's daughter. Knowing that if I refused to allow him to marry her he would do something drastic, I agreed to the marriage. I gave him 7000 rupees to start a cattle business and by the grace of Allah he is doing fine.

Case 2. Farook had wanted to marry Abdul Hamid's daughter, but during that time Farook's mother died. Farook had only one sister and three brothers. Subsequently, a man, Pakir Sa'id, visited Farook's father and said he was interested in arranging a *shallapaddi* marriage between his son and Farook's sister and Farook and Pakir Sa'id's daughter. Farook's father agreed since this would minimize the dowry expenditure for both parties. Farook also agreed, feeling that if he had married Abdul Hamid's daughter his sister would have been left a motherless child without anyone to find a suitable marriage partner for her. His father was an alcoholic, had moved six miles from the village and was incapable of managing the family affairs.

The two couples were married on the same day—August 4, 1978. Farook's wife's dowry included 1500 rupees, two buffaloes, a house and compound, and five bushels of paddy. Farook's sister's dowry include promise to build a house (which was done), brass wares, one cow, one cart and two bulls, and five bushels of paddy. The two dowries were essentially equivalent in value.

Case 3. Aliyar was called "Pottuvil Aliyar" because he was born and raised in Pottuvil, a town on the east coast. His elder brother had married in Kotabowa. Pottuvil Aliyar used to visit Kotabowa to sell dry fish and to buy *ganja*, which he sold in Pottuvil. He was encouraged to marry his brother's sister-in-law, and he had come to Kotabowa with that intention. Plans had been made, but Pottuvil Aliyar felt the dowry was insufficient. The woman came from a very poor family. She was one of six daughters whose parents were separated. Her father lived in Kanulwela and she lived in Kotabowa with her mother, two younger sisters and two brothers. Her mother's brother approached Aliyar about the marriage. Aliyar explained the situation to me as follows:

> I was made to understand this woman's family was doing well so I made arrangements to marry her. They promised paddy lands and many other things. I believed them and married, but now I realize their falseness. They are very poor and didn't keep their promise. Now it is too late.

After the marriage ceremony Pottuvil Aliyar spent most of his time in Pottuvil where he lived with his wife and her sisters, brother and mother. He came to Kotabowa less and less frequently. Villagers were angry with him because he had obtained employment for many of them during the harvest season on the east coast and failed to pay them their money. Eventually he deserted his wife, though his wife expressed a desire to move or go to Pottuvil to find him.

Case 4. This case concerns an elopement which eventually resulted in a double marriage ceremony. Kinship relations are important and have been diagrammed to avoid confusion. This case involves Adam, Haniffa and Sakariya, who were older and married several years prior to Hakkim and Jailan, both of whom were under twenty.

On July 14, 1980 (during the month of *Ramadan*), Jailan and Hakkim had made arrangements to meet Path'Umma and Sitti in the jungle at night. Adam (married to Hakkim's sister) had spotted Hakkim in the jungle and asked him what he was doing. He became suspicious and insisted that Hakkim take him to where the other three were also hiding.

The double affair quickly became public knowledge. For Sitti and Jailan there were no problems because the families were willing to let them marry. Jailan's elder brother was married to Sitti's elder sister and the two families, without incident, decided that the two should get married sometime after *Ramadan*.

In Hakkim's case, his family did not want him to marry Path'Umma. His family knew that the mosque would force a marriage arrangement and so they urged Hakkim to leave for Pottuvil. His family did not want the marriage since the mosque officials could force them to marry and Hakkim would not be able to obtain a fair dowry.

Hakkim asked his friend Hadji what he should do and Hadji replied, "If you leave the village it will be shameful for you and your whole family. The girl may commit suicide. So you should marry her..."

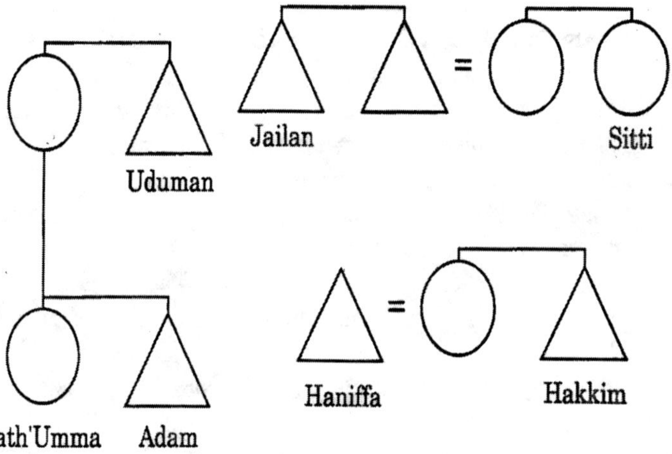

Figure 6. Case 3's Kinship Relationships

Path'Umma's family was anxious for the marriage to be consummated as soon as possible. They insisted that the mosque officials take action on the case since they knew that Hakkim's family was urging him to leave the village. The mosque officials agreed, stating that both should be punished according to religious customs: each should receive one hundred blows with a coconut branch weighing 7 lbs. 3 oz. It was noted during this debate that there were no actual witnesses to the couple's liaison. According to the Koran, there should be at least ten witnesses testifying that they had knowledge that the boy and girl had sexual intercourse. Since there had been no witnesses and both Hakkim and Path'Umma had taken an oath that they had not engaged in sexual intercourse or foreplay, the mosque officials felt that they could not force the two to marry.

It was decided to take Hakkim secretly to Path'Umma. Path'Umma was temporarily staying at her mother's brother's (Udhuman's) residence. Hakkim apparently had no knowledge of this plan and he was led to the house by Adam, Jailany and two other relations of Path'Umma. Hakkim's relations were against the marriage but Adam's relations wanted the couple married quickly that night with the consent of the mosque officials. The mosque officials were to go to the house secretly after *Ramadan* prayers. Haniffa, (Hakkim's sister's husband) had found out about this plan and gone over to Udhuman's house and took Hakkim back to his house. When Hakkim was discovered missing, the mosque officials decided to take Path'Umma to Haniffa's house and force them to sleep in the same house, though in different rooms. Adam considered this situation shameful, but it was the only means whereby the affair could be witnessed. Hakkim's mother then agreed to the marriage if a reasonably sized dowry was provided.

The following day Hakkim and Path'Umma were ritually punished, the whipping being performed by the *Moidenaar* and the lashes counted by the trustee in front of the *Lebbe* and two *Maulevis*. The whipping was neither cruel nor caused bodily harm. Rather, it is meant to shame them and cleanse the miscreants of their sins. The *Moidenaar*, in front of witnesses, takes a small branch and beats them on the back keeping his elbow on the ground, clearly none of the blows could cause physical pain.

The marriage was held at Path'Umma's house. Wedding ceremonies generally take place at the groom's house, but Hakkim's parents were against the marriage. Marriage is usually not allowed during the month of *Ramadan* and for this reason the Muslim registrar of marriages was not called. A *thalli* (a gold sovereign necklace) was given to Path'Umma and Hakkim was presented with five hundred rupees. They were officially registered after the end of *Ramadan*.

Jailan's family was in favor of his marriage to Sitti and both parties agreed to postpone the ceremony until an appropriate time after *Ramadan*. Sakariya, who had been given a house by Califa (see kin diagram) volunteered to vacate the house and give it to Jailan and his bride as part of the dowry. Jailan also received two bushels of paddy and five hundred rupees.

Any rumor or knowledge of an affair between an unmarried woman and man immediately causes problems. The woman's family usually insists on marriage because it is a blot on the woman's and her family's reputation; more importantly, it will be difficult to arrange a marriage for her after such an affair has become public knowledge. The man's family is usually against such marriages because they cannot expect to obtain much of a dowry. The mosque officials always insist that such liaisons, once they become public knowledge (even if they are only the stuff of unsubstantiated rumors), be consummated in marriage. The authority of the mosque officials is legitimized by Islamic law and custom. The officials cannot force a couple to marry, but they can refuse to perform any religious services for the family of the groom and refuse to perform any future wedding ceremony for the couple. Thus, couples, and particularly the man, have no other options available but to leave the village.

All of the parties in this case were relatively poor by village standards. The differences between Jailan's and Hakkim's cases were based primarily on kin relationships. Since Jailan's brother was already married into Sitti's family, he had kinship obligations from both his affinal and consanguineal kin to ensure that his brother would receive a fair dowry and that his wife's family won't be shamed by a refusal of the marriage offer by Jailany's family. Hakkim's family had no such expectation of marriage for none of Hakkim's close relations had married into Adam's family. The expectancies of kinship obligations appeared to be the major causal factor in why one affair erupted into conflict dealt with forcibly by the woman's party and the mosque officials, and why there was no visible display of conflict and no need for the mosque officials to enforce Islamic policies towards the other couple.

Case 5. Razak was coerced into marrying Miriam Bibi by her family one year after he had fathered a child by her. The kinship diagram below notes the relevant relations between the principles involved in this case.

Prior to the marriage, Razak lived with his mother and seven-year-old brother in a small one room house adjacent to Adam Marikar. Directly across the street lived Razak's brother, Haniffa, with his wife and children. Miriam Bibi and her child lived with her parents and two siblings on another street. Hamid, Miriam Bibi's brother, had previously married Razak's sister.

Razak's family occupied a unique place in the village. His father had been an escaped convict and had settled in Kotabowa, he died in the late 1960's. Marikar had taken care of the family since Razak's father had married Marikar's wife's sister. Razak and his brother

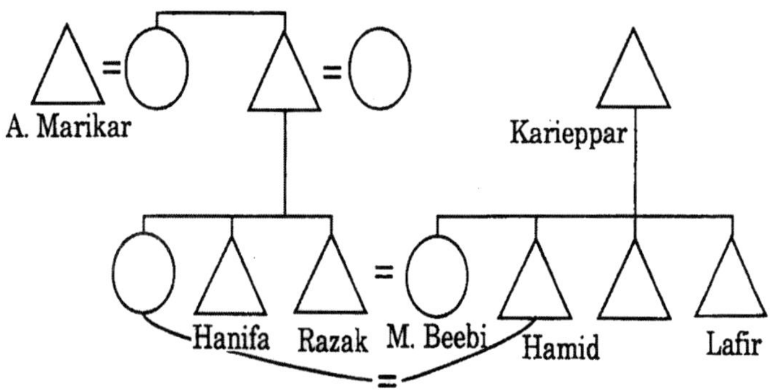

Figure 7. Kin Relations Between Razak and Miriam Bibi

Haniffa were disliked by most villagers and reputed to be crooks who never earned income through honest means. Except for Marikar they had few relations in the village who they could call on for support.

Miriam Bibi's family, the Karieppars, was also poor by village standards, however, they are thought to be the descendants of the ancestral family that founded Kotabowa. The Karieppars have fallen on hard times. Lafir Karieppar worked for me as a cook/servant during my three-year stay. Mr. Karieppar, sixtyish, owned a four bushel paddy field and earned additional income by selling cattle in the village area. All four of his married daughters were married in untypical ways: two eloped, one was caught *flagrante delicto* and forced to marry a poor villager who subsequently died, and Miriam Bibi who, at the time, was an unwed mother with a one year old son.

In December, 1981, Miriam Bibi personally delivered a letter to the mosque explaining that Razak was the father of her one-year-old child. The letter was given to the *Moidenaar* who in turn gave it to the trustee. The mosque officials considered her predicament and requested that Razak appear and explain his position. Razak appeared and admitted that he was the father. A further inquiry was to be held the following Friday after jumma prayers. On the day of the inquiry, Miriam Bibi remained outside the mosque while mosque officials and other interested villagers were inside discussing the situation. Marikar, a relative and supporter of Razak, said the two should be punished but that Razak could not be forced to marry Miriam Bibi since no formal petition had been presented at the time she was pregnant.

Razeek, Karieppar's eldest son, acted as the family spokesman and insisted that a marriage should take place immediately. The Trustee said, "We can only punish them for doing something against the religious code, but we can't compel them to marry. That can only be done if the man wishes." Razak said he would be willing to marry if he received an adequate dowry. Karieppar replied that he was prepared to give two and a half bushels of paddy, five hundred rupees, and promised to build a house with a garden compound. In the meantime, the couple would have to live with them. Razak agreed to these arrangements and to hold the wedding ceremony that night.

After this meeting I talked with Razak in private. He said that Razeek had threatened to "knife him" if he did not marry Miriam Bibi.

One of the Karieppar's was also following him through the day to make sure he didn't leave. Razak's family, in the meantime, secretly made arrangements to marry Razak to another girl immediately following the punishment. Raseek explained his feelings about the situation as follows:

> It is true that I had sexual intercourse with the woman, but she asked me to do it after flirting with me on the street. Thereafter she demanded ten rupees...I offered to marry her before the baby was born, but her family refused, thinking I was a gambler and a rogue. When Razeek Karieppar found a gem they had money, but never considered giving a proper dowry and marriage. Even so, I had committed a great sin and Allah will never let me rest. I am prepared to take the punishment and marry the woman. But her family should be reasonable and give me the necessary dowry...I am prepared to marry. Without it how can I manage my living and take care of the family? In this family not one girl was given in marriage in the proper way and each one is at home without their husbands. The entire family is composed of a bunch of fools without any sense of shame (implying they were all prostitutes). I have been helping this woman, giving her forty or fifty rupees each month. When I asked them to arrange the marriage some time back they refused. Now all of a sudden they want it immediately.

At about nine o'clock that night Razak was led into the mosque, constantly guarded by Razeek, Lafir, and one of the other brothers. At the mosque he was met by the *Maulevi*, Trustee, *Moidenaar* and Marikars. Thirty rupees were given by Razak to the trustee as payment for the punishment. The *Maulevi* asked Razak to recite the following: "I, Razak of Kotabowa, agree to undergo religious punishment and beg Allah to forgive me for the sins I have committed. I promise never to break religious laws again. I promise to live peacefully with my wife and never desert her." He was then taken to a side room reserved for punishments of this nature. Witnesses must be present during the administration of the punishment. The general atmosphere of the room was serious, but not tense or harshly punitive. Razak had a sheepish grin on his face, as if he was embarrassed rather than upset of fearful.

After the punishment was over, Razak was taken outside and bathed by a male age-mate (not a relation) to cleanse his physical body of pollution. This was done in a convivial way with a few jokes and thereafter Razak was considered completely cleansed of his sin. Lafir, Miriam's brother, had a change of clothes for him and, in procession, he was led to Miriam Bibi's house.

At the Kotabowa junction, he visited with his mother and sister who were crying and asking him why he consented to the marriage arrangements. Razak replied that if he did not no one would frequent his tea boutique and it would be impossible to live in the village. All of the people that I queried agreed with this evaluation. Miriam was punished in a back room at home before the marriage registration. She and Razak were both required to pay a thirty-rupee fine which was given to the *moidenaar* for carrying out the punishment. The marriage ceremony was held quickly and Razak paid Miriam one hundred rupees "magar." Magar (a form of bride-price) legalizes sexual access to the woman. On Judgment Day, it was said of those who did not pay *magar* would not be permitted to enter heaven until he paid off his *magar*-debt in hell.

Approximately two months after the marriage, Razak's boutique closed down and Razak was again living with his mother. He seemed confused and lackadaisical, again sliding into poverty. Miriam's family was also upset at his phlegmatic, independent behavior but there was little to do for fear that Razak would eventually desert her completely or request a divorce.

Razak and Miriam Bibi's families were both motivated by a mixture of religious and pragmatic interests. Razak's mother grief was in part motivated by a real concern for how she was going to support her family without Razak. Razak had been the sole provider for the family after his eldest brother married and her eldest daughter had not yet married. Razak had found a gem a few months prior to the wedding and with this money had opened the tea boutique and was, temporarily, well-off. His new found wealth no doubt motivated Karieppar's family sudden interest in the marriage. Razak was caught between these two conflicting interests and also his own moral dilemma, feeling he should marry Miriam Bibi but at the same time felt the Karieppar's were taking advantage of the situation.

Case 6. This conflict over marriage relationships was unusual in that it extended beyond the village boundaries and involved Muslims in the village of Pandaragama, about forty miles to the north of Kotabowa. Neena, a boy of eighteen, had an affair with Mynah which became public knowledge in May 1981. The ensuing problems were still not resolved at the time of my departure in February, 1982.

Below in Figure 8 is a diagram of the kinship relations between the participants.

In May, 1981 Mynah thought she was pregnant. She was of a very poor family and was previously married but her husband had deserted her after three months. Neina, also nineteen and from a poor family, had a marked interest in her. Mynah's family wanted her to marry and made arrangements in May of 1980 for the couple to elope

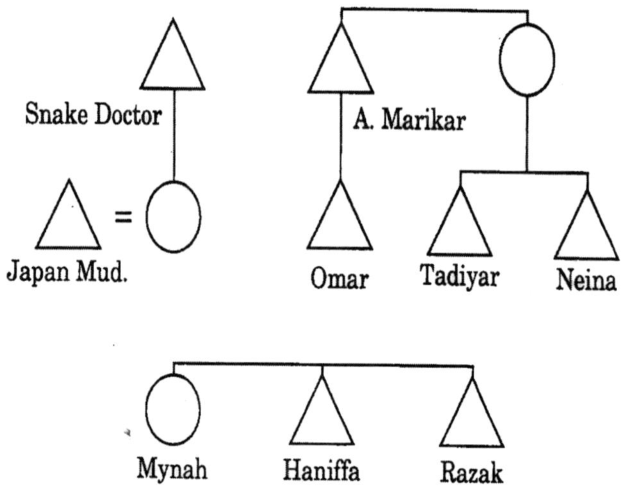

Figure 8. Case 6's Kinship Relations

from the village. Nizar, Mynah's brother, was to contact Neina and, with Adam Marikar and his son Omar (also a *marikar*), the group was to go to Kanulwela to register and legalize the marriage. Marikar's sister was Mynah's mother, and he supported these plans. He was also needed for marriages out of the village must be approved through the mosque. According to the plan, Marikar and Omar were to go first to Kanulwela, a nearby Muslim town, and persuade the local mosque management to perform the wedding ceremony.

Neina's brother learned of this plan and Neina was kept at home under guard and hurried arrangements were made to marry him to an orphaned girl (in the kin diagrams) living with Japan Mudallali. This girl was twenty years old, hefty and tall, but of a very good (i.e., quiet,shy) demeanor. The snake doctor (the girl was his WiSiDa) and Japan Mudallali agreed to pull their resources and provide a dowry of three thousand rupees, a house and paddy lands. They were anxious to see this girl married as she was already twenty years old and had no parents.

Mynah's brothers learned of this counter plan and managed to contact Neina. They gave him five hundred rupees and told him to go with Mynah to Pandaragama. Mynah and Neina walked to Medagama where they caught a bus to Pandaragama. Neina's family was at first uncertain as to where the couple had gone.

The Pandaragma mosque officials had decided to perform the marriage ceremony but insisted that the two be punished according to custom. Just prior to the punishment, Neina left and returned to Kotabowa alone. The marriage plans with the orphaned girl were canceled because of the elopement and another marriage arrangement was made for Neina. In August, 1980, Haniffa, Mynah's brother, petitioned the mosque saying in effect that since Neina had eloped with his sister they must be punished and married. Neina met with the mosque officials and swore that nothing had happened between him and Mynah. Mynah, however, swore that they had sexual intercourse.

That same night, both parties were requested to come to the mosque and swear on the Koran that they had not engaged in intercourse. During the afternoon a verbal dispute had occurred between the mothers of Mynah and Neina. That evening Neina did not appear at the mosque. There had been yet another meeting of Mynah's relations and they had give money to Neina and again urged him to elope. This time accompanied by Mynah's brother, Haniffa, the two returned to Pandaragama. Once more Neina simply disappeared; this time, however, he did not return to Kotabowa but left for Pottuvil on the east coast, where he remained until after my departure in February 1982. It was apparent that Neina could not come back to live in the village without marrying Mynah. There was the possibility that he could marry in Pottuvil, but this would have been difficult since Muslims in that area would have been acquainted with his story and he could not have married any but the most desperate of available women.

"Love" marriages occur most frequently between poor families, often with the woman's family being the poorer and perhaps encouraging, implicitly or explicitly, the illicit affair. "Dracula" for example, had confided that he had encouraged his daughter to attract a boy so that he would not have to pay a dowry and still obtain a good spouse for his daughter.

Case 7. A final example of "love" marriages involved the retired headman's son, Mira Lebbe, and a woman from a very poor family. Mira Lebbe wanted to marry her against his father's vehement protests. They married and resided in Kotabowa and he had received a small dowry: a house and five hundred rupees. Mira's wife died just after giving birth to their first child. Mira Lebbe and villagers believed that the ex-headman had consulted a sorcerer to kill her. Shortly thereafter, Mira Lebbe and his father made amends, there had been no public displays of anger by the woman's family. Approximately a year following her death, Koostapel arranged a marriage for Mira Lebbe with a woman who had been married previously. She was from a very rich gem merchant family in the Badulla area. Mira Lebbe's first wife seemed to have disappeared into the quicksand of history.

The case studies detailed above demonstrate that while the culturally normative model of arranged marriages exists, it is often superseded by more pragmatic considerations. The ideal model is comprised of a constellation of attributes: (1) preference for cross-cousin marriages; (2) preferred range of ages between potential spouses; (3) time when marriage ceremonies should occur, and; (4) relative equivalence in socio-economic status between the households of the two potential mates. There also exist procedural norms for arranging the marriage, the manner in which dowries should be discussed, the ritual performance of the wedding ceremony, etc.. However, the overarching concern of parents is to marry their daughters and sexual attraction often takes priority over these procedural norms.

These case studies indicate the relatively high incidence of "variant" marriage patterns and an explication of the issues and motivations involved. A comparative analysis of love/unscheduled marriages to arranged marriages is presented below. Between 1979 and 1982 I witnessed 22 marriages. Table 6 below summarizes these marriages.

TABLE 6. Types of Marriages

Love/non-traditional marriages	14
Traditional arranged marriages	4
Lack of Data	4
Total =	22

The ideal model of arranging marriages through parental selection of spouses (for their children), which villagers have in their head as a cultural norm or expectation, neither adequately predicts or explains the majority of marriages tabulated above. The model states that the father should arrange a marriage first for his eldest daughter between the age of sixteen and twenty to a cross-cousin (preferably the father's sister's son) and that each daughter should receive, roughly, a dowry of equivalent value. The actual process of selecting marital partners must be understood both in terms of ideal and pragmatic variables. The case studies presented above depict the range of pragmatic and situational factors that should be considered in explanations of the selection process.

Though Kotabowans usually marry for love and/or other pragmatic considerations, this does not mean that kinship is abrogated as a factor. Below, a list of sixty-three couples with the relationship between the bride and groom prior to marriage is presented.

While Table 6 suggests that most marriages are based on the affective criteria of mutual attraction between single males and females rather than the cultural norm of arranged marriages, Table 7 seems to suggest that most marriages occur between normatively preferred cross-cousins.

TABLE 7. Wife's Relationship to Her Husband Prior to Marriage

FaSiSo	22
MoBroSo	11
no relation	23
FaBroDaSo	1
MoSiHuBro	1
FaMoBroSo	1
MoFaBroSo	1
MoBriWiSo	1
MoFaBroDaSoSo	1
FaFaSiSoSo	1
Total	63

Marriage to father's sister's son occurred more often than marriages to mother's brother's son by a ratio of 2 to 1. Both these preferential forms of marriage combined account for 52% of those marriages considered.

Parents prefer to marry their daughter to father's sister's son over wife's brother's son because the father of the daughter, who initiates the marriage arrangement, prefers to give his daughter and her dowry to his own blood. The mother's male relations may not have been relations prior to marriage and the father's affections and focus of interest remains with his consanguines, here his brothers and sisters. The resident pattern of matrilocality also favors marriage preference to the father's side of the family since it will be his relatives rather than his wife's who will be visiting.

However, none of this explains the obvious statistical disparity between these two tables. It would be expected that, as the incidence of love marriage increases, the lack of kin-fit between marriage mates would also increase. Arranged marriages imply that marriages will be arranged between cross-cousins as this is the preferred pattern. In marriages where the parents have control over the selection of mates, cross-cousin marriages would be expected to predominate. Conversely, when this control is lacking, or when "love" and personal choice by singles determines the selection of marriage mates then we would expect a decrease of cross-cousin marriages. The reason for the predominance of cross-cousin marriages, despite the number of non-arranged marriages, is that prior to marriage single males and females related as cross-cousins are relatively "free" and encouraged to flirt with one another and think of each other as potential "lovers." For example, in the circumcision chapter it was mentioned that female cross-cousins were free to visit their *machans* and tease them about their wounded "friend." At bathing spots cross-cousins could tease and flirt with one another. Boys and girls are implicitly encouraged to think of their cross-cousins in sexual terms and they are motivated to meet with them at any available opportunity. The socialization process and context predisposes cross-cousins to become mutually attracted. Furthermore, as will be discussed in the kinship chapter, nearly all one's age-mates, in a kin-based society, are either classificatory siblings or cross-cousins. Though marriages between classificatory siblings occur, they are infrequent.

In Table 8, data has been tabulated from the *Kathi*, which is the village register of marriages. All marriages recorded between Jan. 1936 and May, 1981 have been compiled. It should be noted that marriages between the years 1941 and 1949 were not recorded, for reasons I failed to inquire into at the time. From this data, rates of exogamous to endogamous (in-village, out-village) marriages, dowry size, and the relation between dowry and endogamy/exogamy will be compared.

TABLE 8. Rates of Local, Regional And Out-of-the-Region Marriages Between 1936 and 1981.

	In Kotabowa		**In Region**		**Out-of-Region**	
	female	*male*	*female*	*male*		
1936–49	9	1	4	0	0	**T** = 14
1950–59	19	1	2	2	0	**T** = 24
1960–69	23	4	2	4	0	**T** = 33
1970–79	32	9	6	5	1	**T** = 53
1980–81	25	2	0	3	1	**T** = 31
T =	108	31		16		155

69.3% of all marriages tabulated were between in-village families; 20.0% (31 of 155) were in-the-region marriages; and 10.3% of all marriages were between a villager and someone outside the region. For in-the-region selection of marriage partners, the sex ratio is nearly equal: 14 village males married women in the region and 17 village females married males in the region. For out-of-the region marriages there is a great disparity in this sex ratio: only two village males (both Koostapel's sons) married out-of-the-region females and 14 village women married men from outside the region.

Marrying daughters to out-of-region males is considered a risky proposition and since dowries are major expenses (and investments), families hesitate to speculate their wealth in this fashion. We would expect that in most instances of such marriages, the out-of-region males are poor since the village itself is poor and there is little in Kotabowa to attract outsiders who are relatively well-off. Villagers are aware of the temporary nature of many of these marriages, and hesitate to offer attractive dowries fearing they will be dissipated by the husband after which he will leave his family. For these reasons, predominantly poor villagers with daughters who are difficult to find mates for will consider marriage proposals by out-of-region males.

To determine whether or not a correlation exists between dowry size and selecting a mate from in the village or out of the region, I tabulated statistics of marriages between 1960 and 1981. One would expect that paddy lands in particular would not be provided since paddy land, as opposed to money, is a permanent source of recurrent income. If the husband sold or mortgaged the paddy land, this loss could never be replaced whereas money is a transient commodity and, in any case, is expected to be spent by the husband. The wife's family is always able to earn cash but not paddy land. I have categorized dowry payments into two categories: full payment (i.e., land and cash) and none or partial payment (i.e., land or cash but not both).

In the village and vicinity, out of a total of one hundred and three marriages, there were twenty cases in which no dowry or a partial dowry was provided (20% of all marriages). Of the sixteen out-of-region marriages, there were twelve in which no dowry or partial dowry payments were made (75% of all such marriages). This data is organized into a two by two table in Table 9 presented below.Of the four out-of-region marriages with full dowry payments, two represented the ex-village headman's sons who married women in the Badulla area and received, by village standards, extra-ordinarily large dowries.

TABLE 9. Relation of Spousal Natal Residence and Dowry Payments

	Full Dowry	None/Partial Dowry	
In Village/ Vicinity	80	23	103
Out-of-Region	4	12	16
	84	35	119

Below the non- and partial dowry payments for both the village/vicinity and out-of-region marriages are tabulated to compare whether or not there exist difference in the patterns of partial payments.

There were proportionately fewer inclusions of paddy lands in marriages with outsiders relative to in village/vicinity unions: only two

Table 10. Partial and Non-Payment of Dowry

Village and Vicinity		Out-of-Region	
money (rupees)	*paddy lands* (bushels)	*money*	*paddy lands*
501/	-	501/	-
-	5	301/	-
-	-	-	-
-	4	401/	-
160/	-	-	4
501/	-	-	-
501/	-	-	-
401/	-	-	5
501/	-	-	-
-	7	3000/	-
-	5	1001/	-
2001/	-	1000/	-
500/	-		
-	2	total = 6 total given = 2	
-	-	total—no dowry = 3	
-	-	total—partial or no dowry = 12	
-	5		

total = 8 total given = 8
total—no dowry = 4
total—partial or no dowry = 20

out of twelve (16.7%) received paddy lands compared to eight out of twenty (40%) for those within the village and vicinity.

Conclusion

The data shows that while there is greater variation and individual freedom involved in the selection of a spouse than is normally assumed (see Yalman 1967), there are other cultural factors that constrain the impact of the high frequency of "love" marriages. First, most such marriages occur between preferred relations anyway; and second, the size and kinds of resources given in dowry depend on who the daughter marries. The high risk of marriages to outsiders militates against providing them with substantial dowries. Marrying cross-cousins is preferred because it minimizes the risk on the investment. Kotabowans view marriage selection and the dowry as much in terms of "investment" as in terms of "alliance" or "descent".

THE BURDHA FESTIVAL

The *Burdha* festival occurs just prior to the Islamic month of *Ramadan* (July–August). It is the only festival that is unique to the village in the sense that it is put on by the villagers in behalf of the entire village. The *Burdha* festival differs from other religious festivals held in the village for it is not expressly associated with any saint or Islamic event, it is of recent origin (beginning in 1914) and it takes place in only a few Muslim villages in Sri Lanka.

The *Burdha kandhoori* (i.e., festival) is the most elaborate and costly festival held in the village. The pivotal figure is the *Moulenaar*, a term used to identify those people who claim direct descent from the Prophet. The *Moulenaar* was a large, rotund man in his early fifties; he spoke English and was a businessman in the southern tip of Sri Lanka (from the town of Dikwela). The *Moulenaar* was a very congenial man who seemed used to wielding authority. He explained the origin of the festival to me as follows:

> My grandfather's father started this work in 1914. Earlier there were no *Burdha Kandhooris*...in those days there was no religion and people had no knowledge of the proper way of

> reciting prayers so my grandfather would travel to twelve Muslims villages yearly and teach villagers the proper ways of worshipping. The villages, of which Kotabowa was one, would put on a feast to honor him...Being a *Moulenaar* is like a caste...we are from the blood of the Prophet, no? My daughters must marry other Moulenaars, but boys can marry anyone because the blood is passed through the patriline. However, even sons should marry the daughters of *Moulenaar* families. All my six sons did so. People respect me because I am of the blood of the Prophet and through me they worship him.

In Kotabowa the *Moulenaar* is considered and treated as a holy man. However, the *Moulenaar* status is not revered in all places or by all people. Many Muslims, particularly the more orthodox, disparage the *Moulenaars* as religious charlatans with fabricated pedigrees who earn their living by duping the more naive Muslims. While this undoubtedly occurs, this particular *Moulenaar* seemed to take his status earnestly.

Historical Origins

Mr. Yassim, the Muslim *grama sevaka* (headman) of Bakinigehavela, explained the purpose of the *Burdha* festival as follows (in English): "It was intended to revive the Muslim's faith in their religion and also as a way of propitiating saints on a village level." He went on to explain that the *Burdha mowlood* (the set of recitals which accompany the festival) is designed to ward of illnesses and to keep villagers in good health. At the conclusion of the *Burdha* festival, villagers line up to receive the blessings of the *Moulenaar* and to obtain holy water from him which is to be used at times of illness.

Mr. Yassim also explained that such festivals are not held outside the Indian subcontinent. He said the practice of reciting *mowloods* originated in India as an Islamic response to the Hindu custom of reciting verses of the Ramayana and other famous Hindu exegesis. "Our scholars," he said, "thought that our people (i.e., Muslims) were beginning to follow Hindu customs and, in order to discourage this, they began these *mowloods*."

The origin of the festival may also be connected to the infamous Sinhalese and Muslim riots of 1914–15. The riots began in the highland kingdom of Kandy (see map of Sri Lanka) and quickly spread throughout the island. Prior to these riots there had been little reason for Muslims to fear communal enmity. After the riots, however, Muslims began to congregate in enclaves, according to Mr. Yassim, for defensive purposes, fearing a repeat of the earlier Sinhalese attacks. Villagers had, as previously mentioned, also remarked that houses in Kotabowa were purposely set in proximity to one another so that neighbors could come to one another's aid.

Regardless of the actual origin of the *Burdha* festival, there is some sense in the above accounts that it originated as a response to the incursions of Hindu-Buddhist customs and as a means to maintain or revive the Islamic identity of Sri Lankan Muslims.

The Role of the ***Moulenaar***

The role of the *Moulenaar* is central and necessary for understanding the origin and reason for the *Burdha* festival. The *Moulenaar* was believed to possess great supernatural powers. A popular story is told of the time his son had stolen pumpkins from a neighbor's garden. The *Moulenaar* asked his son if he had been the thief, the son replied that he hadn't. The *Moulenaar*, knowing his son was lying, became angry and told him to "shut up." Since that day, villagers say, the *Moulenaar*'s son has been unable to speak.

In 1979, Hamid, a son of Adam Marikar, had attended the festival in the company of Sinhalese. They had been drinking and Hamid began to curse and slander the villagers as "haram kooties" (i.e., pigs). The *Moulenaar* had approached him and told him to leave. Hamid turned shoved him and began to insult the *Moulenaar*. The *Moulenaar* then told Hamid in a loud voice that he would die within a year. Hamid continued to drink, and over the year both his wealth and health began to wane. By February, 1980 he was too sick to leave his bed and his father consulted with numerous charmers to try and "cut" the *Moulenaar*'s curse. Eventually, a Buddhist ex-monk was asked to help. The monk visited Hamid a number of times over a two month period and Hamid's health began to improve.

In conjunction with Hamid's recovery, his father and brothers insisted that he abstain from drinking and that he promise to ask the *Moulenaar* for forgiveness.

It is the magical power conveyed by the *Moulenaar*'s words that people believe in. The belief in the magical potency of words is, perhaps, a cultural universal. In this sense, the *Moulenaar* is not only a medium whose words are heeded by supernatural beings; his words are also infused with magical properties of their own.

Politics and Conflict in the Village Concerning the Festival

In 1980 the *Burdha Kandhoori* was not held in Kotabowa. Villagers said that the harvests were too poor for villagers to put on a festival. The Trustee had also been accused of pocketing funds from the previous year's festival and, consequently, villagers were wary of donating cash and foodstuffs for the 1980 festival. An elderly villager explained that in earlier years outsiders as well as villagers had donated time and money to the festival.

Referring to the villagers reluctance to finance the 1980 *Burdha* Festival he said, "Last year the mosque officials 'played us out.' We asked for an inquiry into the accounts but no one was able to tell us anything, so the entire village completely lost faith in the management of the mosque. Also, this year the people are broke and afraid they will be cheated again."

Hamsa, the mosque treasurer, went over the accounts with me and explained that although there had been a 7000 rupee surplus the year before, much of it had to be spend on expenses throughout the year. He also admitted that much of the money was probably pocketed by the Trustee or other officials who simply came and asked for sums to pay for improvements to the mosque.

The Trustee was also not eager to revive the festival for 1981. He had received unending criticism concerning the 1979 festival and, when asked to invite the *Moulenaar* for 1981, he balked. The Trustee undoubtedly feared that the villagers would complain about his alleged mishandling of festival funds in 1979 to the *Moulenaar* who, should he side with the villagers, could insist that he, Hassan, resign his Trusteeship.

The decision to omit the festival in 1980 was a result of a constellation of factors: (1) the belief that the Trustee had kept thousands of rupees donated for the mosque; (2) the Trustee's reluctance to promote the festival; (3) poor harvests which left the villagers little additional income to spare for a festival; (4) the inability of villagers to organize the festival without the Trustee; (5) and the possible damage to the reputation of the village should the festival not proceed properly.

The 1981 *Burdha* Festival

In 1981 people were actively petitioning for a *Burdha kandhoori*. While the drought had been an excuse for not holding one the previous year, this time the drought became a reason for holding the festival. Villagers said that the poor harvests were a result of not holding the *Burdha* festival, thus making the *Moulenaar* and, by association, the Prophet angry.

The *Moulenaar* had sent a letter to the mosque inquiring if the village was going to hold a festival in 1981. The villagers knew of this letter and insisted that Hassan reply affirmatively. One informant explained, "Somehow or other we must have the festival for without a festival the village is lost."

While Hassan was personally eager to have a festival he was also afraid that the villagers would use the festival as a platform to vent their grievances against him publicly.

In April, villagers were summoned by Nauman Maulevi to discuss whether or not to hold the festival. After *jumma* services on Friday, the villagers who attended prayers consensually agreed to put on a festival. Hassan, the Trustee, was present at this meeting but took no active part in the decisions made. Nauman Maulevi took on the task of organizing the festival. This state of affairs pleased both the Trustee and the villagers. The Trustee was pleased because Nauman Maulevi was the Trustees "marumagan" (i.e., the Trustee's brother's daughter's husband) and ally; the villagers were pleased because they trusted Nauman, who was a school teacher and had received an Islamic education.

A villager was sent to personally invite the *Moulenaar* for the festival while other villagers were sent to visit wealthy Muslims in the surrounding region and request donations.

Prior to the *Moulenaar's* arrival in early July, the villagers were organized into labor groups in order to give Kotabowa a "face-lift."

Streets were cleaned, the mosque repainted, houses spruced up, etc. The women wove colorful mats and set aside money to buy new clothes for themselves and their children.

The *Moulenaar* arrived, by bus, eight days before the final festival day. He slept in the mosque and was invited daily to visit and eat with villagers. His food was placed on a clean white cloth and he was given a cushion to sit on. He was served by the head of the household, the men of the house and invited guests remained silent and sat a discrete distance away until he finished eating. After the meal he would recite a short prayer and then the men would tell them of their troubles and needs, hoping to enlist his aid. On one occasion a girl of eighteen was brought to him after a meal. She stood, head bowed, while her father explained that a boy had promised to marry her but after their affair became known he had denied making this promise. The *Moulenaar* said he would speak with the boy's family, and if her story was verified, he would ask the boy's parents to arrange the marriage between the two. On leaving a household, the *Moulenaar* would be offered a small payment wrapped in a betel leaf.

For the *kandhoori*, the villagers had rented a loudspeaker to play music and announce individual donations given on that day. Goats, chicken, and cattle were butchered for the final day of feasting. The Trustee estimated that more than one hundred chickens, twelve goats and about ten oxen were slaughtered for this occasion. On the day of the feast, there was a short morning service. The street by the mosque was lined with petty entrepreneurs selling costume jewelry, silver and gold bracelets, brass pots and ornaments, saris and sarongs, etc. Outsiders streamed into the village on foot, by bus, in rented vans, private vehicles, and bicycles. It was conservatively estimated that over two thousand visitors came to the festival. Meals were served in large *sabhans* (bowls) around which five or so people sat and ate. Outsiders, particular those of high status, were served first. Only after the outsiders finished their meals did most of the villagers sit down to eat.

After the meal, people milled around the mosque where the loudspeaker was set up. People approached the *Moulenaar* who would "bless" them. A merry-go-round and swings were set up for the children to play on. No games or contests were organized for adults. At this time, lines of people formed with containers of water to be blessed by the *Moulenaar*.

In the evening, after most of the outsiders had left, the *Moulenaar* recited a final prayer or blessing at the mosque:

> O Allah, [he said] let our sins be forgiven for those who are here and for all villagers. All the people want to pray and I beseech you to help them pray. O Allah, we are very poor and uneducated, therefore send us the means to become rich. O Allah, we want to die with lots of merit. O Allah, bless our request. O Allah, give us plenty of rain and good harvests, give many things to our village. O Allah, we hope for an abundance of rain and good paddy and *chena* cultivations. O Allah, we hope for better education and more comforts. O Allah, please grant our requests.

Apparent, of course, in this prayer is the desire that through the *Moulenaar* or because of his presence, the entire community would prosper. The *Moulenaar* left the day after the festival. He was walked by an entourage of villagers as he slowly made his way to the bus stop. Villagers were praising him, but mostly they seemed pleased that the festival had gone so exceptionally well. The excitement of the festival, the presence of a holy man, the day of feasting, of conspicuous consumption, and of being able to display the generosity and 'wealth' of the village to the outside had lifted the spirits of all villagers.

The *Moulenaar* had not only brought with him the promise of health and prosperity, but also a renewed sense of social identity and esteem. Aside from this, the festival was fun. Only after some days when the effects had worn off would the villagers recall the success of the festival and wonder how much of the donated money was pocketed by the Trustee or other mosque officials.

RAMADAN: THE MONTH OF FASTING

Ramadan is one of the five pillars of Islamic theology—along with hadj (pilgrimage to Mecca), *zakat* (charity tax), five time daily prayer, and the recital of the first *Kalimma* ("There is no God but God"). *Zakat* and *hadj* can be bypassed for reasons of poverty. The month of fasting stands out as the most impressive of these pillars since it is a contract between the healthy Muslim and his God to undergo a fundamental hardship for a month as a testimony to his (or her) faith.

Ramadan, the month of fasting, begins following the Arabic month of Sha'ban with the first glimpse of the new moon and ends with the sighting of the following new moon. The Prophet Mohammed advised Muslims not to keep the *Ramadan* fast "...until you see the new moon and do not discontinue the keeping of the fast until you see it again and if it be veiled to you (by clouds) have it measured..."

Muslims are expected to refrain from eating, drinking or even swallowing their own phlegm from sunrise to sunset.

Prior to commencing the fast at sunrise, a villager will say (in Arabic), "I declare my intention of observing the compulsory fast in the month of *Ramadan* this year for the sake of Allah." On breaking the fast at sunset the villager will say, "O Allah! I fasted only for Thee and only with Thy provision do I break it." Fasting is not meant to be an extreme hardship. Muslims who are ill, on journeys, or females who are pregnant are exempt from fasting; as the Prophet said, "there is no great virtue in fasting when on a journey." The purpose of *Nombi*, the colloquial term used by villagers to refer to both the act and the month of fasting, can be listed as follows: (1) for all Muslims, particularly the rich, to experience the hunger and thirst that the poorer Muslims undergo and thus not only to humble oneself (in devotion to Allah) but to increase one's feelings of charity and compassion towards poorer Muslims; (2) to purify and cleanse oneself of sin through worship and by avoiding money-making enterprises. As one informant noted, "The actual fast is complete only when one acts, behaves and thinks like a true Muslim."

Among the many sayings of the Prophet, the following one captures the villagers' perception of *Nombi*: "It is the month of endurance and the reward for endurance is Paradise. It is the month of sharing with others and a month in which the believer's provision is increased." For Kotabowans, the month of *Ramadan* is a month in which all past sins are forgiven and they may start with a new slate, so to speak. This expiation of sin was explained to me as follows, "You can't work during *nombi*...(During the year)...every Muslim in the village earns money by illicit means. The bad blood created by these illicit means is burned off (by fasting) and we are purified of all sins."

During the month of fasting Muslims are expected to give charity to one another. *Zakat*, the obligatory act of giving a portion of one's wealth and distributing it to the poor, and *sadaqat*, an optional form of charity, were not formally distributed in the village. It was said that no one in the village was wealthy enough to give *zakat*. Grains and other foodstuffs were either given or exchanged with relatives as a form of *sadaqat*. Paddy was also given to sisters living in poverty or to one's parents or parents-in-law. This form of giving was considered by villagers to be motivated both by religious decree and by obligations of kinship.

The most important days of *Nombi* are the twenty-seventh day (*Mihraj*) and the last day of *Ramadan* (*Id-ul-fitr*). *Ramadan* is the month that the Koran was revealed to the Prophet by the angel Gabriel: the twenty-seventh day is the day the Prophet was said to have ascended to heaven on a legendary white horse called Baraq.

On *Mihraj*, Pitchai annually slaughtered a bull, distributing the meat throughout the village. Pitchai explained that this was done "...in order to erase all of the sins that have occurred over the previous year." A family member, usually a child, goes to Pitchai's house and is given a pound of meat wrapped in a banana leaf. The head, a delicacy, is presented to the *moidenaar* for slaughtering the animal.

During the month of *Ramadan*, villagers will awaken an hour or so before sunrise in order to prepare the morning meals. These are large meals inevitably including a rice porridge said to fill the stomach for the day. At sunset, rice porridge is cooked at the mosque; children arrive with bowls and the porridge is ladled out by the trustee or *marikar*. Thereafter, the obligatory daily prayers (*Maghrib*) commence with most of the village males attending each of the evening services during *Ramadan* at the mosque. After *Maghrib*, villagers will either leave and go home, hang around the boutiques or remain in the mosque to chat.

During *Ramadan*, the women are brought together for congregational prayers, each evening. Meetings were held at a villager's house; three houses were selected in different parts of the village so that all the women would only need to walk a short distance to attend *Ramadan* services. Services were led by one of the three younger *maulevis* living in the village. The *maulevi* stands behind a curtain so that he will be hidden from view. The services included both the obligatory prayers and a sermon on proper conduct for Muslim women.

Ramadan is a period when Muslims should turn away from the day-to-day working world and turn their minds and hearts to religion. By enduring the privation of fasting they are expressing their commitment to Islam. This test of spiritual commitment affirms the two core values of Islam: obedience to Islamic doctrines and unity between all Muslims (i.e., *Umma*).

Through these actions (fasting and worship), Muslims erase their sins and ensure their future rewards on the "Day of Judgment." There is in Islam a materialistic bend, akin to Calvinist doctrine, that material good fortune comes to those who are steadfast in their religious practices. To fast brings not only spiritual but material benefits.

Ramadan in Kotabowa

Below is an account of the events and activities that occurred in Kotabowa during the month of *Nombi* in 1980 and 1981. The emphasis is on the relation between "ideal" and "actual" behavioral patterns during this month. Disputes and other discordant acts during the month of *Nombi* are of special concern and conversation among villagers. The exigencies of rural life do not lend themselves to long periods of setting down the trappings and problems of this world. Concomitant with the obligatory dictate that healthy and able Muslims should fast during the month of *Nombi* is the emphasis on daily worship. Business, particularly illicit business, should not be conducted during *Ramadan*, nor should marriages take place. Intoxicants should be strictly avoided and ideally villagers should be sexually abstinent not only during the day but throughout the entire month. People should be charitable, kind, avoid gossip and arguments and *zakat* (2.5% of one's wealth) should be distributed to the poor.

Within the village, however, these religious sanctions were neither enforced nor enforceable. Perhaps roughly ten percent of all Kotabowans fasted the entire month in 1981, most of whom were either women or the elderly. Even the majority of mosque officials did not keep the fast the entire month.

During services, villagers were urged to convey the impression that they were behaving according to the above dictates. In one sermon, Nauman Maulevi admonished villagers that "...These are *Nombi* days and when you transport *ganja* and smoke cigarettes Sinhalese and outsiders [referring to neighboring Muslims and Tablik people who visit during *Nombi*] will be under the impression that you smoke and do bad things during *Nombi*. This casts a bad reflection on all Muslims." In essence the *maulevi* requested that if the villagers were going to breach these sanctions then they should do so circumspectly and in private.

On July 14, 1980—the night preceding *Nombi*—there was a special sermon at the mosque on the importance of fasting. Nauman Maulevi, the *lebbe* and the *moidenaar* presided over these services. The turnout for this sermon was dismal and the mosque officials became upset. Approximately thirty-five villagers attended the pre-*Nombi* ceremony. Arrangements for where the women would pray was discussed. Women were expected to attend the services closest to their homes and, Latif's house (at the junction), Siddik's (near the central node) and the *Lebbe*'s house (in the Colony) were selected.

Even on the first day of *Nombi*, a few villagers smoked openly during the day. When others called attention to this, one smoker grinned sheepishly and continued to smoke. Villagers appeared tolerant of individual breaches of these behavioral sanctions. As the days of *Nombi* wore on, fewer and fewer people continued to fast. Men began to hang around the boutiques smoking, chewing betel, and drinking tea. Petty business ventures were started. Villagers questioned one another as to how long they had "nombied." Many villagers, although they understood that they should fast the entire month, thought of the number of days spent fasting as a kind of merit score. Some villagers explained that since their wives continued to fast, their merit accrued to the husband as well. As one villager explained, "if Allah rewards those who maintain the fast how could he punish the husband?"

The routines of daily life seemed much the same, though with some notable differences. No one began clearing cultivation lands or went gemming during this period. Business ventures and disputes were kept backstage for fear of verbal reproof. Attendance at the mosque was much larger, particularly for night services, than in other months. Conversations also focused more on religious topics—stories about the life of the Prophet, his companions's lives, etc.—than would otherwise be the case. Although the majority of men did not maintain the fast, they exhibited a pride in the religious traditions of fasting, comparing it to Buddhism which has no such strictures.

On the twenty-seventh day, the day the Prophet was said to visit both heaven and hell, loudspeakers were rented and set up at the mosque and that religious music and sermons broadcast from Colombo could be played. On this day, Pitchai slaughtered one of his livestock and distributed the meat. It is the day when all sins are expiated, even the sin of not fasting, and many villagers would start fasting again till the end of *Ramadan*.

On the final day of *Ramadan* villagers bathe and dress in their new or finest clothes prior to attending the morning service. In 1980, the women congregated at the village school for the last *Ramadan* service. On entering the mosque the men are greeted by the Trustee and Adam Marikar, who sit in the antechamber, a white cloth spread in front of them. Money is required to be given and is apportioned in three equal shares: for the Moidernaar, the *Lebbe*, and the *Maulevi*. On this day Tamil beggars line the road by the mosque to receive alms and a temporary tea boutique is erected on the mosque grounds. After services,villagers shook hands, blessed one another and gathered outside to chat. Later they visit with relatives, bringing small gifts or food (usually sweets).

Another unique feature of *Ramadan* day is the custom followed by adolescents and many adult females of staining their right hand with a reddish dye made from *Margossa* leaves. It was preferable to draw a crescent moon and star on the palm of the hand, but usually the design comes out mottled. The staining of hand was said to indicate the completion of the fast and more importantly, signifying that one is a Muslim.

Conflict During Ramadan

In 1981 a fight broke out on the final day of *Ramadan*. Nassar, the *Moidenaar*'s son-in-law, said that he saw the Trustee, in the presence of Omar Marikar, pocket the money that had been donated for the *Maulevi*, *Lebbe* and *Moidenaar*. The *Moidenaar* became angry and publicly accused the Trustee of theft. Omar came to the Trustee's defense and, threatening to strike the *Moidenaar*, told him to leave. Omar is a physically imposing man while the *Moidenaar* is old and spindly. The villagers remained on the mosque grounds discussing the dispute. Mohideen (the trustee's elder brother), Nauman Maulevi (married to Mohideen's daughter) and Ibrahim Maulevi appeared and met with Omar and the trustee. After the conference it was publicly explained, by Nauman, that the Trustee had used his own money to break a fifty rupee note and that Nassar had jumped to an unwarranted conclusion. The *Moidenaar* was called and scolded in public by Nauman. The trustee also added that if the *moidenaar* couldn't do his job properly they would replace him. With this the fight subsided; the eventual outcome was that the *moidenaar* refused to work and was replaced by a boy of nineteen who was a relation of Nauman Maulevi (and by extension, the trustee).

In 1981 there had also been a dispute over where the women should pray. A large paddy warehouse had just been erected by Mohideen. Nauman Maulevi and the Trustee had wanted all the women to congregate there for prayers rather than at three different houses. This would mean that the other *Maulevis*, who presided over the services in previous years, would be out of a job in 1981. A dispute occurred at the mosque during the pre-*nombi* discussion of where the women would pray. Foxer, the father of one of the *Maulevis*, argued that it would be inconvenient for so many women to meet at one place and that it was better for them to walk to designated prayer homes within easy reach. Ibrahim Maulevi remained neutral on this issue, though he stood to benefit the most since he would preside over the congregational service.

Foxer's son and the *Lebbe*'s son (also a *Maulevi*) continued to hold prayer services at their respective houses, against the wishes of the mosque officials. This act of defiance and the dispute were not responded to by the Trustee board. Rather, they publicly pretended that these alternative services for women were not being held. Though this dispute was expressed in religious terms, the issues involved matters of income and attendant prestige for those leading these services. The dispute simmered through the month of *Ramadan* but was contained by the religious principles which fostered the argument (i.e., disputes over income and prestige cannot be explicitly justified in the religious idiom, particularly during *Ramadan*). The argument was also mitigated by the fact that the two junior *maulevis* were close friends of Ibrahim and Ibrahim's motives were never questioned. Hence, the Trustee and Nauman Maulevi's argument was expressed in terms of the Islamic postulate that it is best to pray in congregation. Foxer and the *Lebbe*'s argument was based on convenience.

Comparison Between Ideal and Actual Behaviors During Ramadan

Goodenough (1965) criticized anthropologists for confounding what he terms the "ideational order" with the "phenomenal order,"positing that the two present different data pools for analysis. Yet, among Kotabowan Muslims the discrepancy between theory of *Nombi* and its practice does not diminish their perception of one another as "real" Muslims. *Nombi* is an ideological kernel shared by all Muslims which formulates a series of behaviors. This enables some statements to be made concerning the relationship between ideology and observed behavior. If strict social sanctions against breaking the behavioral precepts of *Nombi* existed then we would expect a close "fit" between concept (i.e., *Nombi*), rules (fasting, charity, avoidance of disputes, attendance at prayers, etc.) and behavior to be apparent. The absence, or lack of enforcement of such sanctions, permits a looser "fit" between ideal and actual behavior. A looser fit does not imply a diminished regard for the importance of *Ramadan* and its associative rules for behavior. As mentioned, the *maulevi* impressed upon villagers the need to act in accordance with the ideal model outside the village. Breaches of *Ramadan* sanctions were to be kept within the familiar confines of the village boundaries; and larger breaches (such as economic activities) were to be done covertly.

The three factors listed below partially explain the discrepancy between ideal and actual behavior in Kotabowa:

(1) ethnic minority—Muslims, as an ethnic minority in Sri Lanka have assimilated and adopted "adhesions" from the customs of the two dominant religious systems—Hinduism and Buddhism.
(2) geographical isolation—Kotabowa is a remote Muslim village. Bounded on the east by a large forest and situated in a predominantly Buddhist region, Kotabowans have had few opportunities, historically, to maintain close social and cultural ties with the wider Muslim communities.
(3) absence of strong central authority—Kotabowa lacked a strong central authoritative leader or body of leaders capable of enforcing socio-cultural sanctions. The mosque leaders have limited authority over affairs directly concerned with the management of the mosque. They can punish villagers involved in unlawful sexual intercourse, but this is restricted to unwed villagers and only when a formal complaint is made. Those officials invested with the powers of decision-making and punishment (other than that connected to the mosque) are Sinhalese. Under these circumstances, the relationship between ideology, rules and behavior depend on the individual's capabilities and desire to fit behavior with ideology.

The ability of individuals to meet the behavioral demands of *Ramadan* were correlated with basic demographic factors such as age, occupation and sex. In Kotabowa it was primarily the females and/or aged males who adhered to these precepts throughout the month. Age was less of a factor for females than for males. Males involved in business enterprises or employed as laborers could not fast the entire period. The old, more conscious of their own mortality and free from the responsibilities of providing for a family, had both the time and the motivation to fast. Females, usually at home and given the opportunity to pray in congregation during this month, were also conscientious about maintaining the fast.

The majority of villagers with whom I interacted daily consisted of males between the ages of twenty and forty. This age group was the least committed to fasting for the month. Males in this age group were concerned about the problems of earning a living and obtaining money for the upcoming cultivation seasons. Their concerns were with living; in their old age, they reasoned, they could fast or, if their wife fasted, her devotion also reflected on them.

The loose fit between the concept of fasting, the precepts for behavior and the actual behavior of individuals was permissible in Kotabowa. The fiction of a close fit was important only in the presence of outsiders. Villages obtain reputations in the area. People from Bibile will refer to someone as a "Kotabowan" and, to an extent, the reputation of the village weighs on the actions of each villager. On trips to Bibile (or anywhere outside the immediate area), most villagers will dress in their better clothes, be sure they are neat, and, if they can afford it, smoke cigarettes rather than *bidis* in public. This public display or performance is meant to enhance one's personal reputation but, by association, it also affects the reputation of the village. The importance of "keeping up a front" implicitly affirms Kotabowa as a social unit. The importance of this association, between villager and village, must be intensified when it concerns a core ideological behavioral concept such as *Ramadan*. For to be a Muslim means to fast during the month of *Ramadan* and act in accordance with the aforementioned precepts.

Conclusion

Ramadan is one of the primary pillars of Islam: it is a religious contract of faith between man and God. In Kotabowa the dictates of *Ramadan* were adapted to the circumstances peculiar to the community through cognitive (rationalization, association) and social (allowance of behavioral variations depending on social context) mechanisms.

Ramadan was a period in which the socio-cultural identity of villagers as Muslims and their more regional/local identity as Kotabowan

Muslims was redundantly verified for thirty days. Villagers know that assumptively, all Muslims throughout the world were also participating in the same event. This knowledge expands their pride and ethnic identification in a country where they are the minority. In addition, the differential social limits for appropriate behavior, depending on whether one is in or outside the village, implies an identification with, and responsibility to, the community. Villagers are socially defined by others and self-defined, as "Kotabowan Muslims." Non-*Nombi* behavior was only acceptable within village boundaries. This does not necessarily imply that since villagers think of themselves as "Kotabowans" there is a corresponding increase in social "cohesiveness" or "solidarity." It does, however, revivify the villagers' social identity as a member of the village as well as with the wider Muslim world.

EPILOGUE

The final day of Ramadan marks the end of the seasonal cycle. The following day the cycle begins anew. The villagers rise at daybreak and everywhere are the sounds of the village: the women are at the well throwing down buckets on frayed ropes to collect water for the morning tea and washing, the children begin to wend their way to school, the men are on their way to various destinations. The villagers are a vocal lot, calling to one another from one end of the village to the other. Again you can see the men smoking their *bidis* or both men and women chewing betel leaf. They are no longer dressed in new clothes, but old saris and sarongs.

It is the beginning of a new year. After Ramadan, the villagers are full of hopes and expectations, for they start of with a clean slate. During Ramadan, however many days they fasted, all have tried to comport themselves as best they could—going to the mosque for prayers, avoiding disputes—their minds focused on the eternal verities of Islam.

Old man Marikar walks down the road stopping to flirt with the women at the well. The Snake Doctor holds court at Razak's shop while Pitchai, his mind always on business, is at the junction in his old green shirt and toothy smile. Siddik and Farook, best of friends for the moment, walk arm in arm to clear their *chena* fields adjacent to one another. Hamsa visits his sister and mother who live next door to me and asks them what they need from Bible. The sun rises above the village, it is a new year and one thing is certain—the year will bring changes the villagers can only begin to glimmer, yet the village will endure in its own singular way.

GLOSSARY

[**Note:** The terms in the glossary are defined in the context of this text. I did not rely on any one criteria for spelling these terms. I aimed for consistency rather than adherence to specific phonetic criteria. The letters in parenthesis refer to language: S–Sinhalese; T–Tamil; S/E–Sri Lankanized English words; M/A–words specifically referring to Muslim customs, these words may be either Arabic or Tamil.]

Adee: S–The leasing of paddy land; payment is usually made in equivalence to the number of bushels sown.

Areloo: S–Small hard nut used as a purgative and also as a dye.

Arraci Mahatteya: S–Traditional name for village headman.

Atam Waede: S–System of reciprocal labor exchange.

Baith: M/A–Prayers/psalms recited during religious processions and on ceremonial occasions.

Basnayake: S–Administrator of ***devale*** lands.

Betel: S–leaf used for chewing and in vows.

Bethmay: S–Chief priest of the Buddhist temple.

Bhikku: S–Buddhist monk.

Bidi: S–Poor man's cigarette, made of local tobacco and rolled in Eucalyptus leaf.

Burdha Kandhoori: M/A–Annual festival held prior to Ramadan.

Chena: S/E–Highlands used for shifting cultivation.

Devale: S–Buddhist folk temple for local deities.

Dos: M/A–Verses of the Koran recited in behalf of the dead.

Ganja: S/E–Marijuana.

Grama Sevaka: S–Government appointed village headman.

Hajj: M/A–The pilgrimage to Mecca; one of the five fundamental tenets of Islam.

Hyatt Nabi: M/A–A Muslim deity often equated with both the Buddhist-Hindu deity Kataragama or Jesus Christ.

Id-ul-fitr: M/A–Last day of Ramadan.

Isha: M/A–Fifth and final prayer of the day for Muslims.

Jamaat Tablik: M/A–National movement to return Muslims to the orthodox fold.

Jumma: M/A–Friday services at mosque; analogous to the Christian Sunday services.

Kacheri: S–Government departments.

Kalimma: M/A–the five fundamental tenets of Islam.

Kaliyaanam: T–Wedding or circumcision.

Kapurala: S–Buddhist folk priest.

Katadhi: S–Sinhalese charmer.

Lebbe: T–Traditional mosque priest. Hereditary position.

Maama(i): T–Uncle (MoBro or FaSiHu) or Aunt (FaSi or MoBroWi).

Maghrib: M/A–Sunset prayers.

Mammoty: S/E–wide-bladed hoe.

Marikar: M/A–Officer of the mosque.

Marumagan(l): T–Son or daughter-in-law; also nephews and nieces.

Maulevi: M/A–Islamic scholar and priest.

Moidenaar: M/A–Mosque crier and caretaker.

Mudallali: S–Businessman or shopowner.

Muradhi: M/A–Vow made for protection.

Nabi: M/A–a prophet.

Nelli: T–A hard green fruit the size of a grape; rich in Vitamin C.

Nindagam: S–Feudal entitlement lands.

Nombi: M/A–Refers to both the act and month of fasting.

Ramadan: M/A–The Islamic month of fasting; the month when the Koran was revealed to the Prophet Mohammed.

Ratha: T–Also Datha; elder sister.

Rupee: S/T–Monetary unit of Sri Lanka. In 1980 one rupee was equivalent to five U.S. cents.

Sabhans: T–Large aluminum bowls from which a group of Muslims will eat communally.

Sadaqat: M/A–Voluntary giving of alms.

Seetu: T–Informal group, usually women, who pool money or particular food item each week so that each member can use the entire sum one time.

SLFP: S/E–Sri Lankan Freedom Party; the major liberal party.

Sunnuth: M/A–Acting in accordance with the sayings of the Prophet Mohammed.

Thallappa: S/T–Dough made of kurakkan (i.e., finger millet).

Thalli: T–Gold necklace given at the time of marriage to the bride.

Thavalams: T–Ox-cart caravans.

Toppi: S/T–Skull cap worn by Muslims.

UNP: S/E–United National Party. The conservative party in power at the time of this study.

Vel Vidane: S–Cultivation officer.

Zakat: M/A–One of five obligatory tenets of Islam; a religious tax of 2.5% of one's wealth which is to be distributed among the poor.

BIBLIOGRAPHY

Bailey, Frederick G.

1960 Tribe, Caste, and Nation. Manchester: Manchester University Press.

1977 The Definition of Factionalism. ***In*** A House Divided, M. Silverman and R. Salisbury, editors, pp. 21-36. Newfoundland: University of Newfoundland Press.

Beals Alan R.

1970 Dravidian Kinship and Marriage. ***In*** Symposium on Dravidian Civilization, in the Asian Series, A. Sjoberg, editor, pp. 107-141. Austin: Jenkins Publishing Co.

Brow, James

1978 Vedda Villages of Anuradhapura. Seattle: University of Washington Press.

Dumont, Louis

1953 The Dravidian Kinship Terminology as an Expression of Marriage. Man 54:34-39.

Farmer, Bertram H.

1977 Green Revolution? Technology and Change in Rice-growing Areas of Tamil Nadu and Sri Lanka. Boulder (Colorado):Westview Press.

Leach, Edmund

1961 Pul Eliya. Cambridge: University Press.

Morrison, M., M. P. Moore, M. U. Ishak Lebbe
1979 The Disintegrating Village: Social Change in Rural Sri Lanka. Colombo (Sri Lanka): Lake House Investments.

Nadwi, A.
1971 Saviors of the Islamic Spirit. Lahore (Pakistan): Ashraf Press.

Obeyesekere, Gananath
1967 Land Tenure in Village Ceylon. Cambridge: University Press.

1984 The Cult of the Goddess Pattini. Chicago: University of Chicago Press.

Pieris, G.
1979 The Physical Environment. ***In*** Sri Lanka: A Survey, M. De Silva, editor, pp. 3-30. London: C. Hurst.

Romanucci-Ross, L.
1986 Conflict, Violence, & MOrality in a Mexican Village. Chicago: University of Chicago Press.

Shore, B.
1982 Sala'ilua, A Samoan Mystery. New York: Columbia University Press.

Srinivas, Mysore
1976 The Remembered Village. Berkeley. University of California Press.

Yalman Nur
1967 Under the Bo Tree. Berkeley: University of California Press.

INDEX